Happy reading!

Gil Friedman

Jan '03

How to be Totally **Unhappy** in a Peaceful World

*Everything
You Ever Wanted to Know
About Being Unhappy*

A Complete Manual with Rules, Exercises,
a Midterm, and a Final Exam

BY GIL FRIEDMAN

Sunstar
PUBLISHING LTD.

How to be Totally Unhappy in a Peaceful World
by Gil Friedman
Copyright © 1997 by Gil Friedman
Sunstar Publishing, Ltd.
116 North Court Street
Fairfield, Iowa 52556
ISBN: 1-887472-1
LCCN: 96-069532

All rights reserved. If anyone tries to copy any pages
of this book they are forewarned that there is a
code in the book that will destroy the copying
machine. Believe me, it's not worth it.

Cartoons by Leo W. Chiantelli
By-The-Sea Graphics, Rt.2. Box 1156
Bandon, OR 97411 (541) 347-3121

Photo Credit: Shona Friedman

Readers interested in obtaining further information on the
subject matter of this book are invited to correspond with
The Secretary, Sunstar Publishing, Ltd.
116 North Court Street, Fairfield, Iowa 52556
More Sunstar books at: http://www.newagepage.com

Acknowledgments

I would like to begrudgingly thank Rita Carlson, Amelia Raymond, Alan Sanborn, Alison Murray, and Natasha Wing for nagging, coercing, and badgering me to make changes in the book that would make the material more digestible and the text more readable. Unfortunately, working with me, this was not possible.

My rancorous ingratitude to Paul Tepley for taking out the funniest parts of the book in the name of redundancy, unclarity, and incongruity. In the end, however, all of the above people are responsible, along with my many English teachers who never taught me correct punctuation, grammar, syntax, or style, together with many unnamed others including, of course, my parents, for all the book's mistakes and shortcomings. I alone am responsible for its good points.

Disclaimer

This book is not intended to replace medical advice. If, after reading any part or the entire book, you are still not totally unhappy, seek the advice of your physician. If you go to him or her long enough, and often one visit is enough, you can become hooked on prescription drug(s). These drugs, their cost and their side effects will produce total unhappiness.*

*Disclaimer to the Disclaimer

Since a doctor, a prescription drug, and surgery saved my life, medical treatment is not always harmful. It has added many unhappy years to my life and can do the same for you.

Table of Contents

NEXT, YOU CONVINCE THEM THAT THE PROBLEM IS NOT THEIR FAULT AND THAT THEY'RE VICTIMS OF LARGER FORCES. THAT'S EASY, BECAUSE IT'S WHAT PEOPLE BELIEVE ANYWAY. NOBODY WANTS TO BE RESPONSIBLE FOR HIS OWN SITUATION.

FINALLY, YOU CONVINCE THEM THAT WITH YOUR EXPERT ADVICE AND ENCOURAGEMENT, THEY CAN CONQUER THEIR PROBLEM AND BE HAPPY!

INGENIOUS. WHAT PROBLEM WILL *YOU* HELP PEOPLE SOLVE?

THEIR ADDICTION TO SELF-HELP BOOKS!

MY BOOK IS CALLED, "SHUT UP AND STOP WHINING: HOW TO DO SOMETHING WITH YOUR LIFE BESIDES THINK ABOUT YOURSELF."

YOU SHOULD PROBABLY WAIT FOR THE ADVANCE BEFORE YOU BUY ANYTHING.

THE TROUBLE IS... IF MY PROGRAM WORKS, I WON'T BE ABLE TO WRITE A SEQUEL.

INTRODUCTION

It wasn't easy, but I did it. It was a long struggle, but I made it. I found unhappiness in a peaceful world. You can too! Maybe you already have. In that case, this book will show you how you did it. And if you haven't, it will show you how you can do it. Moreover, no matter how unhappy, depressed, or anxious you are, by reading this book you can become even more unhappy, more depressed, and more anxious. There is no limit to how unhappy you can be. As the great poet Milton said in *Paradise Lost*:

> And in the lowest deep a lower deep
> Still threatning to devour me opens wide,
> To which the Hell I suffer seems a Heav'n.

I have discovered a "few" simple principles with infinite variations. It is not necessary to go through the rules in order. You can turn to any rule or any page, and get material you need to find total unhappiness.

All it takes is a little dedication to follow these rules and you can't miss. There are exercises after each rule to help you apply the rule. You need a chance to practice your way to total unhappiness.

Perhaps a word should be said about the exercises. In one extensive study, it was found that 9,679 self-improvement books had been published since 1945. These books contained 43,237 exercises. After a thorough investigation, the researchers located an 85-year-old woman in Kokomo, Indiana who had actually done two of the exercises, but she could not remember which ones. Let me stress, to reach total unhappiness, doing the exercises in this book is critical. Do not skip any.

I have also applied to these exercises an honored tradition which I learned from my years of reading college texts. This tradition is that the exercises following the rules rarely have anything to do with the text. Those who have read college texts will feel right at home with this. It is a time-honored way to feel frustrated and inadequate.

Much has been written during the last few years on the subject of keeping a personal journal. Many famous and not so famous people have published their personal journals. There is now a spate of books on the market about how to keep a personal journal. For establishing total unhappiness, having a journal—your Personal Unhappiness Journal—could be a big step forward. All the exercises should be done in your Personal Unhappiness Journal. In your journal, record all your defeats, failures and disasters. Don't put anything good or fortunate in it. This will help in your path to total unhappiness. So go out and buy a journal. Buy the ugliest one you can find, perhaps even a business ledger. If you have to buy a journal with a pleasing cover, make sure it's too big or too small. Your Personal Unhappiness Journal will be this book's companion. Together they will offer a sure-fire method for reaching total unhappiness.

I once heard Tony Robbins, a writer and speaker in the human potential field—which I have nothing to do with—say that less than 10 percent of the people who buy a non-fiction book read past the first chapter. Where do these statistics come from? Does someone follow us after we buy a book to see when we put it down? Perhaps there are other more sinister methods. . . .

However, in support of Tony's remark, I have noticed that used books often have underlining only in the first fifty pages or so. At any rate, I hope you will read past the first rule; there is much material here to increase your misery. If you are one of those people who have trouble getting to page fifty of a book, I have designed this book to help you get to page fifty and beyond. Let me stress strongly, I can give you the rules, but you must walk the path. I cannot walk it for you. Total unhappiness is within your grasp. Good luck!

Rule 1:
Focus on What is Wrong in Your Life

To achieve unhappiness, this principle is crucial. If you're a student and you get three "A's" and one "C," bitch to all your friends, family or anyone else who will listen to you about the "C" you were so unfairly given. Forget the "A's." Fortunately most of us had some unhappiness training from our parents. When you brought home a report card with fourteen "A's" and one "C," you were asked by your father or mother (or stepmother or stepfather), "So, why the "C?" Usually your parents focused on what you did wrong. Be sure to follow their lead to achieve complete misery. One of my friends told me that when she asked her mother why she was so critical of her and never told her when she did anything right, her mother replied, "You know when you do things right. It is my job to point out what you do wrong."

The saying about marriage goes, "One thing about being married, your mistakes never go unnoticed." The issue is not that other people focus on what is wrong with you. The real issue is that you focus on what is wrong with yourself. To be totally unhappy this is an absolutely indispensable habit to develop. No matter how much early training you received from others, it is essential that you ingrain this habit. Moreover, in the past and even today you are sometimes complimented on what you do right or on your accomplishments. Discount these comments! It doesn't matter what anyone thinks of you. It is only your opinion of yourself that counts. No matter what others say to you in a positive way, if you have the discipline to continually focus on what is wrong in your life, you can be unhappy.

The corollary to this principle is also a great catalyst to total unhappiness. The corollary is simple: what you focus on will expand. The mind can only focus on one thing at a time. So if you focus on what is wrong in your life, that portion of your life will grow and expand like a cancer. To be unhappy and have your misery grow, always discuss your problems with anyone who will listen until you wear out your welcome. Then you will be able to complain about having no friends! This really works. I know from personal experience. In order to stay totally unhappy, you must keep it up. Unfortunately for staying unhappy, many problems have a tendency to dissipate over time without anyone, including yourself, doing anything. So to stay distressed, you have to keep your problems in focus all the time.

Exercise for Rule 1:

Since it is always urged that we start where we are, let us start with our bodies. Go to a mirror. Look at your body. What don't you like about it? Look for sags, bags, flaps, and wrinkles. Can you pinch an inch? Take note of what bad shape you're in and how old you look. Perhaps take a nude picture of yourself, or have someone take it for you, and place it in your Personal Unhappiness Journal. Repeat this exercise at least every six months. The photos will tell the story and your unhappiness will have no place to go but up.

Rule 2:
Keep the Waters of Your Life
Muddy by Constant Activity

Have you ever stood beside a clear calm pond? You can see insects skimming the surface, plants growing from the bottom, and sometimes small fish darting between the rocks. If you take a rock and throw it in the water, the mud rises up from the bottom and obscures the water. You can also take a flat rock and skip it across the pond. Ripples will extend from each point the rock hits the water, obscuring the surface. This is a great analogy for becoming totally unhappy. Either throw rocks into the water to muddy it or skip rocks across it to obscure your vision. Combining both is a great way to get and stay miserable.

Enough of analogies or metaphors or whatever that was. Let's get down to brass tacks. What do I mean by continually muddying the water? It's easy, be constantly active. We all know that idle hands cause trouble. If you don't do anything, you get bored. It's better to wear out than to rust out. You have to become an activity junky. It's your new drug. Your home becomes a brief stopover to change clothes. Your life becomes crowded with activities and you don't have enough time in the day to get them all in. The result is that your pond is continually muddied and obscured. There is no time for reflection. You are tired, but too busy to rest. Because you are so busy, when new things come up that you really want to do, you can't fit them into your already busy schedule. You try to make every minute count. You take no rest between projects.

As an example, let's say you just finished cleaning out your kitchen cabinets of all the useless things that have been there for years. Not such a simple task for most of us. Okay, you did it. DO NOT REST. Do not congratulate yourself. Do not reward yourself for the good task you accomplished. Before the waters clear, go immediately into your bedroom and start on your bedroom closet. Keep the water muddy and the surface rippled. One of the best ways to keep the waters of your life muddy is to create pressure and excitement. This will be discussed in the next rule.

Exercises for Rule 2:

1. In your Personal Unhappiness Journal, list all of the activities you do in a day— your normal daily tasks. Now see how you might expand these activities and think about what other activities can be squeezed in during the day to give you absolutely no time for yourself. For example, after you finish work and have come home from your aerobics class to eat and change clothes to go to your 12-step meeting, see if you can write a letter to your mother, to whom you haven't written in eight years. After writing three lines, tell your mother you don't have enough time now, but you will continue the letter later. Put the letter away. After you come home from your meeting, search for the letter.

2. If you are near finishing a major project, such as cleaning out the garage—a foreign land you haven't looked deeply into for years—immediately decide to organize

your desk. It doesn't count if your documents were sorted within the last four years. Keep working until you hate your desk and your life, or are totally exhausted. Quit only then.

Rule 3:
Stay in a State of Pressure and Excitement

We all know it is better to be excited than to be bored. Although it is hard to be excited about ordinary things all the time, there is a way you can get excited about anything, and that is to create pressure. Pressure is, for many of us, the equivalent of excitement. If you have a 2 P.M.

appointment and can get there on time, then there is no excitement. If you can relax at all on the way over, there is no pressure. However, if you go to your appointment at the last minute and you have to drive fast and watch out for the Highway Patrol, the pressure builds. This excitement is a drug. After getting hooked on it, you need larger and larger doses to keep it up.

Perhaps the place we crave excitement most and get it the least is in our relationships. In the beginning all romantic relationships are exciting. Meeting the new person, seeing what will develop, the chase, the union. But after several years together (or sometimes a weekend), most if not all the mystery is gone and all the things you most loved about the person, you now find annoying and boring. In a sense you could say that most good marriages are boring. It is the same pattern and rhythm, day in and day out. This just doesn't create the excitement that is necessary to be miserable.

As George Santayana, the modern philosopher, observed, "It takes patience to appreciate domestic bliss; volatile spirits prefer unhappiness." For unhappiness, patience will never work. You crave excitement, whether it be a new partner or an affair. We have expressions for this such as the "seven-year-itch" and the "mid-life crisis."

You have to have excessive excitement for total unhappiness. You have to create it any way you can. If you are a student, you must wait until the last minute to study for an exam. Excitement is created by having to read 300 pages of Chaucer in one night. If you do your own income taxes, do them the night of April 15th. Then you can race down to the post office at midnight to have the stamps postmarked so you won't have to pay the penalty. That really gets the adrenaline flowing. Exciting! And while you are going through this you not only feel unhappy but very intense.

Perhaps the difference between the

excitement we like and the excitement we don't like is whether we feel we are responsible for creating it. If you decide to go mountain climbing and it turns out to be dangerous and exciting, you would probably be happy because you knew that it was your idea. But if you study for an exam or do your taxes at the last minute, you feel that this pressure and excitement is forced upon you, and you feel miserable. Therefore, to maintain unhappiness, you must continually create pressure in your life and feel that this pressure is caused by an outside force. In no way are you responsible. Another good way to create pressure is to disrupt the rhythm in your life. This is discussed in the next rule.

Exercises for Rule 3:

1. Tomorrow morning just before you leave for work, see if you can squeeze in mopping the bathroom floor. It hasn't been cleaned in ages. This might make you late for work, but it will also cause a lot of pressure and excitement as you race to work.

2. Get a stopwatch and time your daily tasks such as making the bed, eating breakfast, washing dishes, driving to work, peeing. See if you can do them in less time next time.

3. Buy an appointment book. Starting with the moment you wake up and continuing until you go to bed, fill in all the time slots in 15-minute increments with things to do. Be sure not to allow time for contingencies or interruptions. Look at it throughout the day to see how far behind you are and how many things you have not accomplished.

4. For a week, try doing absolutely anything and everything that is requested of you by your mate, children, employer, employees, friends, and especially charitable organizations. Do this regardless of all your other obligations. By acquiescing to everything without any regard to your own presently committed obligations and time, you will create an incredible pressure in your life.

Rule 4:
Have as Little Rhythm in Your Life as Possible

You've seen a child jump rope. She has to jump rhythmically or she trips. Rhythm is a uniform recurrence of some activity. On earth it is the change of seasons, the ebbing of the tide, the turning from day to night. In your own life there is also a rhythm, although it is sometimes not quite so apparent. You arise each morning at the same time, dress, meditate, exercise, have your breakfast at a certain time. After work when you arrive home, you have dinner at a certain time, do some evening activities whether it be a weekly card game or sports event, etc. Whatever you do, if you do it on a regular and persistent basis, you create rhythm in your life. But for total unhappiness, the less rhythm in your life the better. Who wants to be in a rut? Someone once observed that the only difference between a rut and a grave is the depth.

Having a rhythm creates repetition. Who in their right mind likes repetition? Learn to do things a different way each time! Get up each morning at a different time. Go to bed at a different time. Make each day as different as possible from the one before. Keep yourself hopping. Keep changing. The less rhythm in your life, the more unhappy you become. I do not speak from books. I know this to be true from the school of hard knocks.

If you have been going to a yoga class for a while as part of your routine, use any reason possible not to go. For example, your aunt Tilly calls and you haven't talked to her for a long time. Don't tell her you'll call her back so you can go to your class—after all she's old and might die before you return her call. Be sure to rationalize: it's just one time. When the next class takes place, it will be easy to find another excuse and shortly the rhythm of your yoga program will be broken. The next way to increase your unhappiness is to constantly compare yourself to others.

Exercises for Rule 4:

1. Don't go home after work or when you normally do. Stay away from home until just before bed time.

2. Set your alarm one hour earlier than you normally do.

3. Don't buy any groceries for at least a week.

4. Skip brushing your teeth before you go to bed, but on an irregular basis.

5. Don't turn off your TV at night when you go to bed. Leave it on all night. Waking up in the morning to the blaring banality of morning TV is especially conducive to unhappiness.

6. Don't turn off your TV any night to read that book that has been sitting on your shelf for over a year that you're "dying" to read.

Rule 5:
Always Compare Yourself
with Others

Comparing yourself with others is a wonderful way to reach unhappiness. It is especially helpful to compare yourself with others who you feel are doing better than you. By doing this you can continually put yourself down.

For example, I am a graduate of Harvard Law School. Now that is pretty impressive, but it is easy to nullify using comparison. To begin with, I was one of the students who made the top half of my class possible. In fact, I may have been one of the students who made the top three-quarters of the class possible. But I did graduate. I even wrote a book on the law and taught law. Yet, when I open the alumni magazine and look in my year's class notations, I can't compare myself to my peers, who have sent in announcements of ascendancy to Chief Operating Officers in large corporations or have been elected to some high governmental office. Recently, I didn't even have to check the alumni magazine as one of my classmates, Janet Reno, was appointed Attorney General. What have I done compared to these fellow classmates? It's a great way to keep myself down.

When I compare myself to my fellow classmates, I feel too much like a total failure. Sometimes to ease my pain, I turn to the obituary column to see who bit the dust. "At least I am still alive," I tell myself. At least I have outlived some of those brilliant classmates.

Remember there is always someone richer than you, thinner than you, wealthier than you, and healthier than you. By focusing on what you think others have instead of what you have, you can keep yourself in a state of total dejectedness. It doesn't pay to compare yourself with anyone you think might have or be less than you. "What's the big deal about that?" The comparison with people you feel are doing better than you serves two important functions on your path to unhappiness. One is that it makes you keep striving to obtain goals that others have: a new Mercedes, a bigger house, or a better paying job. The second is to prevent you from enjoying what you presently have.

Comparison and envy of what others have is like an acid that keeps you from enjoying life. Therefore, by constant comparison with others, you can keep striving for things you don't have and be dissatisfied with what you do have. After you get the things that you are striving for, you will find that there is always someone who has more. This outlook will keep you striving for the new goals and keep you from enjoying what you have obtained. While we are on this subject of acquiring things, we come to the interesting area of getting things in general and our consumer society. This will be discussed in the next Rule.

Exercise for Rule 5:

In your Personal Unhappiness Journal write down the names of at least four people from your grammar school class who have better jobs than you, earn more money than you, live in bigger houses than you, and have better looking or smarter mates than you and who have "made it." Do the same for your high school class and your college class. Read these lists over at least once a week and brood over it. Then look at what you have and see how inadequate it is compared to what others have.

Rule 6:
Consume as Much as Possible;
Produce as Little as Possible

When it comes to consumption, the simple truth is that no matter what we buy, the happiness it gives dissipates very quickly and soon vanishes. Then we go out and look again for what we think will give us happiness. We go on yet another shopping trip, looking for the "new" something that gives us the thrill of novelty. If you're a woman, life may become a recurring trip to the shopping mall to amass closets full of clothes that are worn briefly and forgotten. If you're a man, life may become a recurring trip to hardware or sporting goods stores to get more toys that end up collecting dust in the garage. This constant consumption is guaranteed to be a slow, steady road to total unhappiness.

The one thing you should avoid for total unhappiness is producing things. Why create a greeting card when you can buy one? Why plan a party when you can have a caterer do it? Why cook a decent meal when you can easily pick up a hamburger and french fries at a fast-food place in a couple of minutes? (Perhaps you have stopped cooking entirely. It is a badge of independence to show that you don't have to cook.) The result is that you have become a total consumer: it's buy, buy, buy—shopping trip after shopping trip— mall after mall. As you know, after a day of shopping, you're exhausted.

A man used to be able to go into his garage in the evenings and weekends to work on his car. With the advent of modern cars, with their greatly increased complexity and computers, this method of productive behavior has been largely eliminated. This has resulted in only two major areas where people feel they are producers and can be creative.

The first area is gardening, which is probably the leading hobby in America, and the other is woodworking. Growing one's vegetables or woodworking is not usually economically sound on a dollar and cents basis. E. B. White, the famous editor of *The New Yorker*, once wrote an article on what it cost to raise his Thanksgiving Day turkey. When he added up the cost for the shed he built, the fencing material, the wire mesh for the pen, the food, etc., the bill came to $400. And the same could probably be said if a hobbyist wood-worker figured out all the equipment, cost of materials, etc. to build a desk that you could buy ready-made for a few hundred dollars at a discount furniture store.

Anyone who has tried his or her hand at writing, even if he or she gets published, knows how little financial compensation there is in writing. On a financial basis, writing is the only profession in which after you "make it," you still haven't "made it." So if you write, do it purely on the basis of dollars and cents, unless you want to take a chance on not being entirely unhappy. Only do what gives you immediate cash, something that it "pays" to do.

To sum up, keep buying things and produce nothing on your own. It's a sure method to dejection and gloom. And if you keep buying things, you will also enter the financial debt nightmare. This is discussed in the next rule.

Exercises for Rule 6:

1. Don't hold onto your old car. Even if it's clean, reliable and excellent transportation. Obviously, it's not trendy. So go out today and buy a hot little sports car or a spiffy four-wheel drive sport utility vehicle or a BMW with the custom interior and sound system topped only by Carnegie Hall. Thanks to interest, the car will cost you an additional 50 percent or more of the sticker price by the time you have actually paid for it. But so what! Just think how bad you'll feel writing out the checks for full coverage car insurance, personal license plates, and the monthly payment. For more details on how to finance your new car, read the next rule.

2. In your Personal Unhappiness Journal list all of the things you want to buy. Spend at least one day on your weekend shopping for some of these items. When you buy one, go back to your list and add the next item you want to buy.

Rule 7:
Get and Stay in Debt
—the More the Better

To become and stay totally unhappy, there is nothing quite like the bill collector knocking on your door, receiving threatening letters, and receiving phone calls at work and all hours of the day and night pressuring you to pay off your debt. There are many ways for you to get in and stay in debt. One of the most popular methods these days is using your credit card and not paying it off each month. Perhaps you think the idea of paying 16, 18, or even 21 percent interest is crazy. It is, unless your goal is to get and stay miserable.

There are many people whose payments on their credit card balances don't even cover the monthly interest charges on their account, so even though they make a monthly payment, the amount they owe each month goes up without even adding any other purchases to their cards. And they wonder why they can't get out of debt. If you charge $2,000 on a credit card and pay only the minimum amount due, usually $10, it will take over thirty years to pay it off and you'll pay more than $8,000 in interest. Is it any wonder you keep receiving credit cards in the mail? So for total unhappiness buy everything on credit and let the interest accumulate. As the saying should say, "Buy now, suffer later."

Above all, do not open a savings account and start saving on a regular basis—no matter how small the amount may be. Have a vague plan that some day you're going to start saving after paying off all your debts. You will find that you never have any money left to save. As one of Parkinson's laws points out, "Expenditures rise to meet income," so no matter how much your income increases, nothing remains to be saved. For financial chaos, don't pay yourself first by placing some of your earnings in savings and live off the remainder. And speaking about savings, the next rule about being unhappy is to have big desires.

Exercises for Rule 7:

1. Suppose you have just received in the mail a "Certificate of Guarantee" telling you that you are a "Ten Million Dollar Finalist." You are guaranteed a prize. All you have to do is dial the toll-free number and answer a few questions. After answering the questions, all you have to do is wait for your prize. Why wait? To paraphrase a New Age saying: "Spend the money and the money will come." Go down to your nearest shopping mall and start spending your future winnings. Continue to buy until the present ceiling on all your credits cards is met. Don't worry about comparative shopping and prices. You will get the money as sure as the sunrise follows the night. If the money doesn't come, you will reach a new level of unhappiness that you didn't think was possible. You could always consult with a bankruptcy attorney. If you won't go this route because of your timidity, there are less extreme avenues

discussed in the next two exercises.

2. Never pay the cost of an item you buy on credit within the one month interest-free period. Instead, pay the smallest amount the credit card company allows.

3. When buying large items, such as cars and homes, always take the payment plan over the most years possible to increase how much interest you pay. As for cars, never recognize that the fragrance of a new car is the most expensive fragrance in the world.

Rule 8:
Desire More; Be Less Content with What You Have

I DON'T HAVE A THING TO WEAR!

Buddha was reputed to have said that there are two things that can break your heart. One is not to get your heart's desire, and the other is to get it. What did the Buddha know, anyhow? Things were a lot different 2,500 years ago—what could people have desired then? They didn't have electricity, indoor plumbing or even black and white TV. Desires are wonderful! Without them, why even get out of bed in the morning? Desires motivate you. They are the engine to our whole economic system. Where would we be without them? A few desires are good, and a lot of desires are even better! If you have big desires you will work hard, borrow, cheat and even steal to get what you desire. You could become obsessed with your desires.

If your desires are very big and formidable, even unrealistic, such as striving to be a pro basketball player when you are 5'2", or making billions in the stock market before age thirty, they will be achieved only at a very big expense, in terms of financial resources, health and personal relationships. By striving for improbable goals, you will find that what is not achieved contributes to total unhappiness.

There is another philosophy that

argues that the way to happiness is to reduce your desires to a minimum and be content with what you have, to enjoy the moment and not get involved in chasing after what you do not have. Those who have tried this—and I am certainly not one of them—experience very little unhappiness. This is also the argument of the couch potato. Who wants to be a couch potato? The way to melancholy is to have as many desires as possible and preferably desires that take a tremendous amount of effort and resources to obtain. This leads us to the next rule in our search for unhappiness. Always focus on the desire, not the means we use to get it.

Exercises for Rule 8:

1. In your Personal Unhappiness Journal write down a list of all your desires. Do not let any slip your mind. The next day see if you can add to your list. The bigger the list and the larger the desires, the better.

2. If you have obtainable desires, see if you can expand them so that you will only achieve them with great difficulty.

3. Review your list each night and realize how far you are from reaching your desires. Contemplate the inadequacy of the things you have in your life. Regular practice will eventually lead to complete discontentment with what you have. Remember, it takes practice. Only a few lucky ones can achieve profound unhappiness in just a few sessions.

92

Rule 9:
Keep Your Focus on the Ends, Not the Means

An essential ingredient for unhappiness is to constantly focus on the goal and not the path. As the old cliché goes, "The ends justify the means." By keeping your focus on the ends, and not the means, you will do anything to obtain your goal. It will not matter how badly you treat others or yourself to obtain your goal. You will suffer all sorts of unhappiness in mind, body and spirit as you pursue the carrot in front of you. When you feel your body in pain trying to tell you to slow down or stop, ignore it. As the saying goes, "No pain, no gain."

If your personal relationships become more and more stressed as you pursue your carrot, just realize that these people in your life don't understand you, and don't recognize that what you are doing will really benefit them in the long run. Achieve the goal at all cost! And above all else, it is detrimental to achieving unqualified misery if you enjoy yourself on the path.

You must ignore Dr. Karl Meninnger's remark that "work" is where the ends are important and "play" is where the means are important. What do psychiatrists know, anyway? It doesn't matter how much you dislike what you are doing, if you are doing it to earn your living, you realize that you have to put up with it. Whoever said that work should be enjoyable? Most people hate their jobs, no? If you really enjoy your work you might feel guilty for having a good time and getting paid for it. You also might feel less unhappy. This leads to another interesting facet for unhappiness and that is the whole question of giving and receiving in relationships with others. This will be discussed in the next rule.

Exercises for Rule 9:

1. Even if you do what you like to do, it is possible to do it in a way that leads to total unhappiness. Take gardening for example. Never do it in moderation. When you garden, do it until it hurts. Suppose, during the Spring, it was hard to get any time to work in your garden because of the weather. Therefore, on a day when you can garden, work all day long without any break. Do not wear a sun hat, nor a visor, nor garden gloves. These things are for dilettantes. Your

goal is to get it all done in one day. If God made the Earth in six days, you can make your small garden in one. Do not go inside your house until it's pitch dark outside and you can no longer straighten up. Then, as you come into the house completely bent over like a hinge, complain loudly to anyone who might be there, or anything if alone, "Oh, my aching back. It's killing me." You will not be able to garden or get around much at all for a few days. When you finally can straighten up, you will hear the call of your garden. Immediately repeat the exercise. Eventually this leads to permanent pain and the inability to do your favorite activity, gardening. Lest we forget, this brings complete misery. It will take some time, perhaps years, but many gardeners have done it, and you can do it, too.

2.   In your Personal Unhappiness Journal write down all the things you don't like about the path you are presently on.

Before going to sleep, retrace your actions of the day. Take note of how insignificant, meaningless, tedious and thankless simple daily tasks can be. Record any frustrations in your Personal Unhappiness Journal.

3. Also in your Personal Unhappiness Journal, create a new list and see what actions you can take to increase what you don't like about your life. Try to add at least one thing a day, or at least each week, that you don't like about your life. This will help increase the pain and discomfort you feel in your life. A few examples may be useful as guides. If you are married and have a child, and are not getting along with your spouse, try having another baby. You will find it really works. If you bought some rental property in the hope of having a good investment and discover you just don't like the hassles of being a landlord, buy another rental unit. Adding depth to your problems almost infallibly will lead to more

misery. I'm sure you can think of areas in your own life to add to your pain.

4. Find a mildly competitive recreational activity like 4D basketball for out-of-shape adults. Play each game as though it was the NBA playoff final. Pay no heed to others' or your bones, tendons, and ligaments. Remember, only winning counts.

Rule 10:
Take as Much as Possible;
Give as Little as Possible

Much has been written on the subject of giving and taking. It is not possible to cover the subject in its entire philosophical, emotional and spiritual aspects here. For total unhappiness, however, one basic principle can be clearly delineated. The idea is straightforward: look out for Number 1 and to hell with everyone else.

John F. Kennedy was wrong when he uttered, "Do not ask what your country can do for you, ask what you can do for your country." Rubbish! For total unhappiness, always look for what is in it for you. If there is nothing in it for you, why do it? Charge as much as you can for anything you have to offer. Why give anything away? You're not a sucker. You had to go to school or be trained to learn what you do. Now you must get your "investment" back. This is especially true if you really hate what you are doing, but it works in all situations.

If someone asks you a question, and it would just take a minute of your time to answer it, why do it, if you won't be getting something immediately back from the person who asked it? What are you, a charity outfit? If a panhandler asks for a handout on the street, why give it? He or she is a bum who should be working and is just going to take your money and buy booze. And if you give to one, you might never stop and will soon go broke. Never, ever give! Look away as if the person who asked is invisible. It takes practice, but you'll soon become pretty good at it.

In areas of your life where you do give, make sure you get credit for the giving. The more credit the better. Your name should appear on a list or in the newspaper. Your generosity should be announced far and wide. Never give anonymously. And if someone asks for some of your time, give as little as possible or none at all.

Above all, give very little to yourself. You don't really deserve it anyway. If there is an activity you like, but doesn't pay you in cash at least as much as you normally make, why do it? You're no fool. Why grow carrots when you can buy them cheaper in a grocery store? Why build a cabinet when you can buy a ready-made one for a few dollars at a discount furniture store? Why give yourself time to relax when there are so many goals to accomplish and so many desires to satisfy? Ignore the Roman philosopher Cicero's saying "Unless a man can sometimes do nothing, he is not really free." No, don't give others or yourself even the right time of day, unless of course, there is something in it for you. And that something should be tangible. Money is always best. Taking and not giving is a wonderful way to not only achieve a Scrooge-like existence, but total alienation from others as well. This brings us to the next topic of discussion, the rule on how we deal with others.

Exercises for Rule 10:

1. Whenever someone asks for anything, invariably ask "What's in it for me?" If you can't find any financial reward or won't get some kind of official recognition, don't do it. Never spontaneously agree to give without making this analysis.

2. The first exercise applies even more strongly to anything you want to give yourself. Never do anything for the pure enjoyment you might receive from it. Always look for what you can get out of it in terms of money or recognition. If you can't find financial benefit or some prestige, skip it.

Rule 11:
Take Everything Personally. Take Offense whenever Possible

As you are quite aware, the center of the solar system is you and not the sun. Copernicus was thoroughly incorrect. The only reason he determined that the sun was the center of the solar system was that he, unfortunately, did not have the opportunity to meet you. A mere ten or fifteen minute conversation with you would have left no doubt in his mind, that you are center of the solar system and the universe as well.

Whenever anyone does anything which is connected to you in any way, the main reason is for its effect on you. These people may sometimes not be aware of it, but it is nevertheless always true. For example, if you have an appointment with someone and he is late, the only reason for his lateness is because he knows how upset you become when you have to wait. There is no other possible reason for his tardiness. Any person who keeps you waiting surely thinks you just don't count and are not worth being on time for. Therefore, you are perfectly right to take offense at him for being late, even if only a few minutes. Start getting angry at him. Harshly judge this unreliable wretch, and vow never to make an appointment with him again. Remember all the other times he has kept you waiting. By the time he does arrive, you should be so mad at him that it will be obvious just by looking at you. You should be in such an angry state that you cannot enjoy anything you planned to do together. You are totally in the right. He is totally irresponsible. On no account should you ever bring anything to read while waiting for an appointment as it could distract you from taking offense at anyone's tardiness.

If you are single and have a date with someone and she calls up and cancels it, the only reason she is doing it is because she knows how much you will be hurt by it. What other possible reason could she have? Except perhaps that she found someone better looking than you, or smarter than you, or with a brighter personality than you. You are perfectly justified to take offense at this behavior.

If your spouse or "significant other"

wants to go camping, and you don't like camping, the only reason your spouse decided to go camping is because it annoys you. You are perfectly warranted to take offense at this decision. I mean for what other reason could he or she want to go camping? God, doesn't your partner know that you don't like to go camping? Use this as an opportunity to get into a big unresolvable fight so you can be even more miserable while your partner is gone.

If you have teenagers who are out later than the agreed-upon time, the only reason they do this is because they know how much it upsets you. A teenager has no other legitimate reason for staying out beyond the agreed-upon time than to offend you. In fact, it could be argued that the only reason teenagers do anything is that they know it upsets their parents. This actually may apply to almost all children's behavior. Parents have the right to take offense at their children's behavior, no matter what they do.

In conclusion, the more offense you take at people's actions and the more you show it, the more unhappy you become. This rule can be applied wonderfully to all work situations and business dealings with others. This will be discussed in the next rule.

Exercises for Rule 11:

1. Each night before you go to bed, review your interactions of the day. Was anyone rude to you? Did anyone ignore you or take you for granted? Reflect on how people invariably slight you.

2. In your Personal Unhappiness Journal list all the specific things your spouse or "significant other," parents, children, friends, employer or employee have done or not done to upset you. Read over this list at least once a day and feel the anger for each of the acts.

Rule 12:
Assume that in Business Relationships the People You are Dealing with Have No Respect for You. So, as a Defensive Measure, You Should Have No Respect for Them

Suppose you are a tenant. You must realize that all landlords are slumlords. They do not give a damn about you. They only want your money to pay off their mortgages and then retire in the lap of luxury on a Miami beach. Therefore, why take care of the apartment? Let it go to hell. It's not yours, right? If you have a cat, even against the landlord's wishes, let it piss on the carpets. You might have to smell the urine, but you'll only be there a few months or maybe a few years. The carpets were poor quality anyway. If a pipe springs a slow leak, why tell the landlord? He probably won't fix it, and if he does, he will then raise the rent. To hell with him.

If you are a landlord, you know how worthless and shiftless tenants are. Why provide a nice and decent place to live? It's "just a rental." In a tight housing market, you can just about rent anything in any condition anyway. Why bother to spend money making any improvements? You can always rent the place regardless of its condition, right? And if you make it nice, the tenants will certainly destroy it. Always buy the cheapest replacements you can. Tenants love to have a hot pink toilet with a lime green seat to go with their lavender bathtub and tangerine sink. I suggest that when tenants get together, they tell landlord stories, and when landlords get together they tell tenant stories. If you are a tenant, see the landlord as the enemy. If a landlord, see the tenant with enmity. Friction is sure to follow in your relationship with each other.

If you work, see your boss as an exploiter. Without a doubt he or she is someone who will always try to get the most out of you with the least pay possible, and who continuously cuts the meager fringe benefits you have. Therefore, give the least of yourself you can possibly give. Featherbed your job whenever possible and steal anything you think you can get away with.

If you are an employer, remember that all employees are an ungrateful bunch who will get away with as much as possible. Never trust them any further than you can throw them. Never consult them about any work-related decisions. Treat them as a necessary evil until you can replace them with a machine or move your plant to some "third world" country (industry's newest coping trend). In Brazil or Indonesia, you can pay wages at a tiny fraction of what you pay American employees, plus you do not have to bother with working conditions or worker benefits. Moreover, you can pollute the environment with impunity.

If you're a shopper, remember that all stores sell shoddy merchandise at outrageous prices through manipulation and false advertising. Retailers inevitably mark the prices up then reduce them to the regular price. Then they advertise this regular price as the sale price. Consequently, it is perfectly okay to rip merchants off any way you can. For instance, when grocery shopping, leave the carton of ice cream that you decided not to buy on the shelf with the crackers. Don't return it to the freezer section. So what if it has completely melted by the time a clerk discovers it. It is also a good idea to nibble from the bulk food bins, and leave your grocery cart where a car might hit it. A great way to exact revenge in a department store is to mess up the clothing racks as you try on dozens of different outfits. Be sure to leave anything you don't buy strung out on the dressing room floor. It's a big store, right? They can afford it.

These are just a few examples of business relationships that contribute to total unhappiness. I'm sure you can think of others. One area of personal relationships which is the most conducive to misery is marriage. This will be discussed in the next rule.

Exercises for Rule 12:

1. Review your business dealings of the past week. Look for hypocrisy and greed from any other person you were forced to deal with.

2. If you're a tenant, list in your Personal Unhappiness Journal all of the ways your landlord is taking advantage of you: high rent, doesn't fix things, doesn't appreciate your deep love of loud rap music and doesn't like your pet boa constrictor.

3. If you're a landlord, list in your Personal Unhappiness Journal all the ways your tenants take advantage of you: paying rent one day late, objecting to your unannounced inspections, expecting you to keep the toilet working every day, wanting the freezer to keep their Ben & Jerry's ice cream hard, and griping when you look at their mail.

4. If you're an employee, make a list of all the ways your employer is taking advan-

tage of you: low wages, unsatisfactory working conditions, inadequate vacation pay, expects you to run personal errands on your own time, objects to personal long-distance calls at work, and imposes his or her moral values on you by prohibiting drinking at work.

5. If you're an employer, make a list of all the ways your employees are taking advantage of you: not working hard, goofing off whenever you turn your back, complaining about working overtime every week, wanting retirement and health plans, expecting loyalty after only thirty years of working for you, and guilt tripping you about a layoff six months before retirement.

Rule 13:
Keep in Mind that Your Spouse, "Significant Other" or the Lack of a Spouse or "Significant Other" in Your Life is Responsible for Your Unhappiness

To paraphrase the great American philosopher Ralph Waldo Emerson "Is not marriage an open question, such that those who are married want to get out, and

those who are not married want to get in?"
The reason that those in marriage or relationship want to get out is that they find something seriously wrong with their partner. They are certain that getting rid of their partner will get rid of their problem. Those not in relationship think that something is seriously wrong with themselves and if they get a partner they will become happy. Both rationales are ideal for total unhappiness. Your partner or lack of a partner is the reason you are unhappy. What could be clearer than that?

To stay totally unhappy when you have a partner always focus on her or his shortcomings and failings. Dwell upon how much better off you will be without her or him. If your mate does anything good for you, keep in mind all the crummy things (s)he has done in the past. The occasional nice thing can't possibly balance all the wrongs that they have inflicted on you. If for any reason your beloved should criticize you for anything—and it has been observed that one thing about being married is that your mistakes never go unnoticed—immediately fire back what is wrong with your mate. Keeping your loved one's list of faults in the forefront of your mind greatly facilitates this. For example, if she tells you that your car is blocking the driveway and she can't get her car out, immediately respond with, "You never want to make love anymore!" If he complains that the clothes you just bought are much too expensive for your budget, respond quickly with, "You are such a slob. You leave a trail of clothes everywhere," or, "You couch potato. You do nothing but watch sports on TV."

One especially good technique for staying unhappy in relationship is to remember that your partner is "below" you. Think of all the people you could have married and should have married. Your husband, your "knight is shining armor" turned out to be a "knight in rusty armor." Your princess, the girl of your dreams, turned out to be the fat lady in the carnival. Without question your partner is not good enough for you. Tell anyone who will listen to you just how low he or she is.

Another trick for creating marital acrimony is learning which buttons to push and precisely when to push them to get your partner going. For example, the wife will say something to the husband such as, "You're late. Again!" She knows her husband will respond sharply—then the rest of the "conversation" goes on automatic. Once the statement is made, retorts from "B" to "Q" just fall out of their mouths without a thought behind them.

To achieve total unhappiness if you are single, you must focus on all that is wrong with your single state: how lonely you are, how you eat alone, how you have to sleep in bed by yourself, etc. Then obsess about all the things that will become right once you have found a partner: someone to wake up with, someone to watch the sunset with, someone to rub your back, and so on. Keep in mind that by being single you are desperate for a partner and any partner is better than none. For real wretchedness believe you are not lovable and deserve only to meet losers.

To insure unhappiness, it is important to forget what was wrong with any previous relationships. If the other person broke up the relationship, be sure to block out any problems that you had with it. Focus only on what was good in past relationships so you can continually eat your heart out about them. When discussing relationships or lack of them, a book on unhappiness would not be complete unless we discussed sex, which will be covered in the next rule.

Exercises for Rule 13:

(A) Exercises For Those Presently in Relationship:

1. Fantasize about the perfect mate for yourself. If you don't know what you want, just see what you have and imagine the reverse of it. Someone once defined marriage as a process of finding out what sort of guy your wife would have preferred. Robert Schuman once observed about his fantasy, "When I was a young man, I vowed never to marry until I found the ideal woman. Well, I found her—but alas, she was waiting for the ideal man." For sinking into depression, these fantasies are wonderful.

2. On small, separate pieces of paper, write down all the traits that are wrong about your "significant other." Place these notes in a cookie jar. Every morning pull out a thought. Throughout the day refer to your selection for the day and remind

yourself how truly irritating and frustrating this flaw is.

3. If you have been in a relationship for less than six months, make a list of all the things you like about your mate. Six months later you will be able to go back over the list and place "do not" before the word "like" on most of the items. In another six months you will be able to put "do not" before "like" on the rest of the items. Moreover, you will have added many new items to your list.

4. No matter how long you have been in a relationship, try to change your spouse to be more to your liking. If your mate won't change willingly, nag. Do not ever give up your efforts to change him or her. (S)he needs your help, whether (s)he likes it or not.

5. Discuss with your divorced friends how much better you would be without your present partner. Recently separated friends will give you much support for

getting out of your present relationship.

(B) Exercises For Those Not Presently in a Relationship:

1. Tell yourself why you're alone. Linger on the fact that no decent person could possibly find you lovable.

2. In your Personal Unhappiness Journal, list all that is wrong with your present unattached state, then list all the wonderful things that being in a relationship would bring you. Read these lists once a day. Add at least one thing to each list every week.

3. Forget all the problems you had in your last relationship. Immediately suppress any that come to mind.

4. In your Personal Unhappiness Journal list all the good things about your previous relationship. This may be difficult at first, but the longer you are not in a relationship, the easier it will be to make

this list. Read this list every day. Add at least two items a week.

5. Get into a relationship as soon as you can—with anyone willing to have you. Any relationship is better than facing yourself alone each day.

Rule 14:
In Sex, Make All Sorts of Impossible Demands on Yourself and Your Partner

There are endless sexual demands you can make on yourself and your partner. Unfulfilled sexual demands are an excellent way to establish and maintain your anguish. A demand guaranteed to bring misery is the demand that both partners should reach orgasm simultaneously (or at least within five seconds of each other). Since for most couples this has about as much frequency of occurrence as Halley's comet, this goal will keep you miserable and constantly frustrated with sex.

There are other means to keep each partner unhappy in sex. The man can assume that the woman will have an orgasm on demand using the same approach and techniques in an identical sequential order each time—lips for 2 minutes, breasts for 2 minutes, then bingo! This approach has the added benefit that it will encourage the woman to fake it. As the woman becomes more involved in acting out a role to please the man than in expressing her true response, she gets tired of faking it. Eventually the man realizes that the woman isn't a professional actress. Throughout the entire process, the woman can feel worried that something is wrong with her. After the man figures it out, he can then feel rejected because he is not good enough to give her an orgasm.

Speaking of being "good enough," there are two beliefs that lead to deep despair for a man. I highly advise that any men in search of "depth" unhappiness ingrain these two beliefs. You must be able to have an erection anytime, anywhere, no matter what. And if you ever have a premature ejaculation, from then on it will happen every time you make love. These two beliefs are the high road for men to utter failure and despondency.

Likewise a woman can achieve "depth" unhappiness. One essential belief is that you are not a real woman unless you have an orgasm while a man is inside you. Other fundamental beliefs for failure include feeling inadequate if you need oral sex, manual stimulation, or masturbation to reach orgasm. The golden rule for women that always promises unhappiness: whatever feels good, you can feel guilty about it because your mother would never approve.

Sex is a great way to mutually achieve distress. After all, misery loves miserable company. As you and you partner stay together, you can both be discouraged because the frequency of times you make love decreases. Demanding that the frequency continue at the same rate as at the beginning of a relationship is a foolproof method of staying unhappy. As the saying goes, "If you put a nickel in a jar every time you make love during the first year of your relationship and then afterwards take a nickel out every time you make love, the chances are you will never get all your nickels out." While this doesn't apply to all couples, wishing that your sex life stays the same as when your romantic involvement began three, ten or twenty years ago, is a wonderful way of staying stuck in the past and missing today's blessings.

One final point about sex: never be friends with your sexual partner, especially with your spouse. It is too messy and confusing. This brings up the next rule concerning friendship.

Exercises for Rule 14:

1. If you're married and having sex, fanta-size about the person you'd really like to be having sex with. If you actually are making love to that person, fantasize about having sex with your mate. In your mind never be with the person you're actually having sex with.

2. In your Personal Unhappiness Journal, list all the demands you make on your-self and on your partner in order to have "good" sex. Note how seldom they are ever met. Brood over it. Never discuss your list with your partner.

Rule 15:
Have as Few Friends as Possible, Preferably None

For total unhappiness, the paucity or complete lack of friends works wonders. Not having anyone to discuss your misery with makes you even more unhappy. Men are much better at not having close friends than women. Therefore, it doesn't surprise me that one of the reasons woman live on the average eight years longer than men is that they have more friends.

Before you make new friends, consider all the negative aspects of friendship. To establish friendship takes time. As we have said several times before, "time is money." Can you afford the time from your busy schedule for something so unprofitable as friendship? Friendships that you develop because you hope to get something back from the person are not friendships, but business relationships. Business relationships are also great for developing total unhappiness, provided you always keep in mind your expectation of something in return, if not today, then sometime in the future. This is the sort of "friendship" politicians develop with hundreds, if not thousands of people. The politician who claims he has hundreds or thousands of friends probably doesn't have a single one.

Another negative aspect of friendship is that you often have to go out of your way to establish a friendship. Perhaps your potential friend is a person who rarely phones or visits you. This means that you must do all the calling and visiting, although once you call or visit, you have a good time. Well, why should the burden always be on you? If you call or visit once, that person should call or visit the next time.

If you already have an established friendship, it takes time and effort to maintain it. If you don't cultivate it on a continuous basis, it withers. However, in a deep enough friendship, you can be out of contact for years and when you do get together, you and your friend talk as if you had seen each other the day before. Most intimate friendships take years to cultivate; some often start in childhood. You can see why you wouldn't want to develop this kind of friendship if you are truly bent on being unhappy.

When you make friends at work, these people may seem like great friends, but the moment one of them leaves the job, no contact will be made again. These friendships of convenience, although not as strong as an intimate friendship that follows you through your life, are still not a good idea for reaching total unhappiness.

There are three fundamental techniques you can use to prevent forming any friendships. The first is to lay out all your problems and troubles as soon as you meet someone. Take your potential friend into your confidence immediately and tell them every gory detail of how unhappy you are. Tell your potential friend about your lousy relationships, your dysfunctional family, your present and feared future illnesses, and especially your financial woes. Second, do all the talking. The less time you allow your possible friend to talk, the more certain you can be that no amicable feelings will develop. If this person tries to get a word in edgewise, cut him or her off immediately with such phrases as "Let me interrupt you," or "Let me finish my sentence." Third, ask for favors as early as possible after you meet. Perhaps he wouldn't mind lending you his brand new car. Or she wouldn't mind baby-sitting your two children while you go out on a date. Be sure to explain to her, "Well, you hardly ever go out yourself, so it really isn't a burden on you." She'll love you for your candid assessment of her life.

One last point: not only should you have as few friends as possible, you should also keep your acquaintances down to the bare minimum. Acquaintances are not friends, but at least you acknowledge each other when you meet. For our purposes, let us say anyone who you address by their first name is an acquaintance.

Let's say you live in an apartment house and every day when you return home another tenant arrives at the same time and shares the elevator ride with you. This has been going on for a while, and you have never introduced yourself. Well, don't. Nothing could be more dangerous to your unhappiness then to introduce yourself and begin exchanging "hellos" or some small talk. Furthermore, it's hard to remember names. What if you introduce yourself and the next time you meet, you can't remember your neighbor's name. So embarrassing. Other bad things can happen, too. Perhaps that person will come knocking on your door some day to borrow a cup of sugar or vodka. Perhaps he is actually coming to "case" your place. Also, remember that acquaintances can become friends. Who needs that?

Recent studies show that when neighbors know each other by first name there is less crime in the neighborhood. For your total unhappiness you want to live in a high crime area, don't you? So it's best to live in an apartment house for years without knowing any other tenants. The same applies to neighborhoods. It's the American way. Remember, not only friends but any acquaintances are dangerous to your unhappiness.

Exercises for Rule 15:

1. In your Personal Unhappiness Journal, write down all the times you needed your friends and they weren't there, all the times you did favors for your "friends" that were not reciprocated, and all the times your "friends" forgot your birthday while you always remembered theirs.

2. Make a list of all your "real" friends: people you can really open up with and share your real concerns and joys, not just acquaintances or people you are friendly with for the hope of getting something from them now or in the future. If you have no "real" friends, congratulations! You do not have to do any further exercises for this rule. You are well on your way to total unhappiness.

3. If all else fails and friendship is forming despite following the above rules, ask your potential friend to loan you money. Ask for a few hundred. There is no sense piddling around and asking for a ten dollar loan. If your potential friend is crazy enough to loan you the money, do not pay it back when promised. Always have an excuse and try to borrow even more.

4. Determine that you won't contact your friends until they contact you first. If they do contact you, demand that they do some favor for you for all you have done for them. If they refuse, drop them.

5. Look over your list of friends. Do any of them make less money than you or in other ways have they not "kept up" with you? Drop them. You can't afford to hang around with people who have not "made it." It will reflect badly on you. It will also detract from your ability to attract more successful people you can use in some way.

6. Make it a goal to eventually have no friends; then there will be no demands on your time.

Midterm

Just in case you have not been paying close attention, it is time to check up on you. Simply reading without practice won't work on the path to total unhappiness. Therefore, it is time to test yourself.

1. Discuss in detail the content of the first forty-eight pages of this book. Do you agree or disagree with the author? If you disagree with the author, write out a forty-eight page rebuttal. If you agree with the author, write out a forty-eight page agreement. Make sure all the sentences are correctly punctuated and the grammar is correct. Be concise. Neatness counts, too. Do not look back to the first forty-eight pages. This is not an Open Book Exam. This question is worth 38-1/2 points.

Send your rebuttal or agreement to the author in care of his publisher. In a few years, he'll look at your answer and send you your grade.

2. You have an appointment at 2:00 p.m. It is now 1:30 p.m. It will take you approximately twenty-five minutes to get to your appointment. You should:

   a. Go directly and peacefully to your appointment so you are sure to get there on time and even have a few minutes to spare.

   b. Leave now in a rush. Drive very fast, watching for the Highway Patrol in your rear view mirror. Naturally, you arrive ten or fifteen minutes early. Because you're early, it is guaranteed that the person you have the appointment with will show up at least fifteen minutes late. Because you rushed out, you forgot to bring reading material with you. While you wait, fume that this person is totally worthless and is not worth making an appointment with ever again. Assume that person doesn't think much of you to keep you waiting. What other possible reason could they have for keeping you waiting?

c. Knowing you have plenty of time to get there, go check the oil in your car and the air pressure in the tires. Refill if necessary. Then check the windshield washer level and the radiator coolant level. Refill if necessary. This should take about 20 minutes by the time you clean up. Then leave your house and speed to your appointment watching in your rear view mirror for the Highway Patrol.

d. Leave at 1:30 p.m. and do a couple of errands on the way. After the second errand, it is 1:50 p.m. and you only have ten minutes to get to your destination. Drive very fast watching in your rear view mirror for the Highway Patrol.

There are three correct answers for the path to total unhappiness. Each gets 10 points. If you answered "a" as correct, drop 53 points from your total unhappiness score.

3. When you buy your next car, you should:

   a. Stretch your payments over as many years as possible, preferably five or more.

   b. Don't pay attention to the total cost of the car (determined by multiplying the amount of the monthly payment by the total number of payments). Only pay attention to the cost of the monthly payment.

   c. Always accept the price listed on the car window sticker. If it's printed there, it must be the price or why is it stated in "black and white?"

   d. The best way to check a car out is to kick the tires. If your foot bounces off the tire, it must be a good car. Why else would so many people do this?

All the choices for this question are correct. This is really a trick question because even if you picked none of the choices, there is no way you can lose on your path to total unhappiness when buying a car. There should be at least one easy question on every test, no? You get 10 points for each answer selected or not selected.

Exam evaluation:

If you got 90 to 100 points, you are totally unhappy. Congratulations! Read on to fine tune your misery. If you got 60 to 90 points, you are mildly unhappy and obviously have to sharpen your skills. Any score below 60 indicates a person with happy feelings. If this is your score, you know you have a lot of work to do to achieve total unhappiness.

Rule 16:
Search for Something Outside Yourself that Will Make Your Life Complete

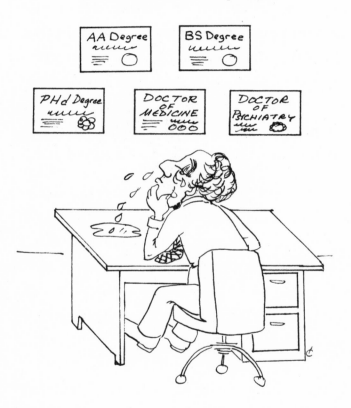

T he search for "the thing" that will make your life complete is one of the best roads to unhappiness. You can waste years, spend all your money, and burn out your brain trying to get this "thing." The thing can come in all sizes and varieties. Some of the usual ones include: the right relationship or getting out of your present one; getting a better job or getting out of the one you have; or getting a degree, whether it be a BA, MA, Ph.D., LL.B., etc. Other great "things" could be owning your own home, or a bigger home, a smaller home, or a summer home. Two more good ones are: getting out of debt or finding a new friend.

The list can go on forever, but to achieve total unhappiness you need to pursue at least one thing that you don't have now in order to make your life "right." It must be a thing that will make everything wonderful. All your unhappiness will end and you will enter the land of bliss and remain there in perpetuity. Fortunately for staying totally unhappy, you will probably never get that desired thing. Even if you do get it, you will find it won't make your life complete. You will look for the next thing you need. Which brings us to the next

chapter: Never do what you enjoy doing
until after you do what you should do.

Exercises for Rule 16:

1. In your Personal Unhappiness Journal,
   make a list of the hundred most important things you need to bring into your
   life to make it complete.

2. In your Personal Unhappiness Journal,
   make a list of the hundred most important things you need to eliminate from
   your life to make it complete.

3. Review these lists daily.

Rule 17:
Never Do What You Enjoy Doing until after You Do What You Should Do

Never doing what you enjoy doing until after you do what you should do is a terrific way to achieve unhappiness. Most responsible people feel that they should only do what they like to do after taking care of their "obligations." A housewife might wait to read a book until finishing all the housework, the shopping, the errands, the cooking and the care of children. A man who wants to play tennis might feel he should play only after he has done his weekend chores. Chores are endless. Doing all the chores first is a brilliant strategy to achieve a state of full unhappiness. You are usually so exhausted after doing all that should be done, that no energy is left to do the enjoyable things. Chores are a wonderful double-edged sword in your unhappiness quest. If you only do the chores you feel you have to do, you resent those chores because you don't have the energy do the things you enjoy doing. If you do the things you like to do, you can't enjoy them because there are so many chores you have to do.

Some examples might clarify the idea. You might want to play with your child, but there are dishes in the sink, so first wash the dishes. If there's time, you'll play with your child. You might want to take a photography class, an area you love and want to learn more about, but you're too behind on your chores at home. When you get your chores up-to-date, then you'll take the class. This principle also applies to bigger things in your life. If you're a budding novelist and have a regular job, never get up an hour earlier each day to work on your novel. What could you accomplish in an hour? If you are working for your degree, never take time out to do the things you enjoy, just study. When you get your degree, then you can start doing the things you enjoy. This leads to the next rule on being totally unhappy. Realize that life is a serious business. There are no unimportant decisions.

Exercises for Rule 17:

1. In the morning, ask yourself what one thing you would enjoy doing this day. Then counter this thought with at least five other things you should do this day. When was the last time the toilet bowl was cleaned? How about your closet? Are there cobwebs in the corners? When was the last time you called your mother?

2. Whenever you are on the verge of doing what you like to do, start feeling guilty and immediately reflect on all the things you should do. Do these things before you do the thing you like. Do the things you should do until you are exhausted, or there is not any time left to do the things you like to do.

Rule 18:
Take Everything in Life Seriously. There are No Unimportant Matters

When looking around the world, how can one not take things seriously? What is there to take lightly? Life is a serious business. Everything matters—what clothes you wear each day, where you go to for dinner, what movies you see, the color of the bathroom's hand soap dispenser—each of these decisions must be treated seriously.

Nothing should be treated casually. Never look at your decision from the vantage point of the future if you want to be miserable. You must always feel the pressure of the moment and the importance of your decision. Nothing is inconsequential. Each decision requires long, careful deliberation. For example, always inspect the menus of four or five restaurants before you sit down for dinner. Eating has significant consequences for your digestive system, your spirit, your pocket book, and the relationship between you and your dinner partner.

I am an expert in using this rule. Everything I do is critical. When I bought a bicycle helmet, I searched every store in town to get the best helmet at the best price. Although it can be argued that this is good, you must go beyond any reasonable point in your search for utter unhappiness. You must fear making a mistake so much that even making decisions over relatively small matters is difficult. Remember, there are no small matters. Your future depends on it.

Decisions such as which restaurant to go to or which bicycle helmet to buy eventually get decided. I mean you have to eat. And if you ride a bike, you realize it's best to have a helmet, although apparently many people don't agree. Always remember, deciding on one thing causes you to miss out on something else, and there's always another decision around the corner to keep you continually unhappy. Another way we can stay miserable is the subject of the next rule. That is, not to laugh about anything.

Exercises for Rule 18:

1. Contemplate the consequences of making a wrong decision. Consequences tend to escalate like the domino theory of Communism in Southeast Asia. Bear in mind that one mistake, no matter how small, can lead to many.

2. For each decision, write a list of all the reasons why this decision is so important in your life. Constantly mull over these reasons.

Rule 19:
Laugh as Little as Possible, Never without a Good Reason

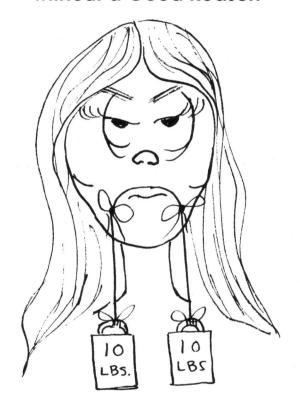

As discussed in the previous chapter, life is a serious business; it is anything but a laughing matter. If you're thinking about laughing, before you do, consider the following: do you have a good reason to laugh? Laughing without a good reason is just plain irresponsible. Look at your present financial situation. That's probably pretty funny, but is it a good reason? Certainly not. Better yet, you might look at your sex life. That could be very funny, but is it a good reason? Of course not. Only irresponsible and frivolous people laugh at these things. In order to laugh you should be happy. If not, you're a hypocrite. There is no place for laughter when your goal is abject misery. Ignore comments such as "For God's sake, lighten up." You must grimace your way through life.

Many places are inappropriate for laughter. You wouldn't laugh at a funeral, would you? This is a serious matter, no? (The Irish seem to have a good time at funerals and the big parties afterward, but what do the Irish know about unhappiness?) Weddings are not an appropriate place for laughter, either. Weddings are a serious matter, although at present, weddings don't seem to be as permanent as funerals. Neither are birthday parties, which mark another year closer to the end. Not a laughing matter. Definitely not. For complete unhappiness, there is no place for laughter. You need a sense of humor to laugh, and a good belly laugh without any use of the intellect is no way to become despondent.

One of the most dangerous things about laughter is that it is contagious. Once a person starts laughing and really gets into a big belly laugh, it is worse than a cold virus and could easily infect anyone in the room. Therefore, not only should you laugh as little as possible, but you should also stay away from people who laugh. They are dangerous to your emotional state. Avoid exposure to comedians, funny movies, funny books or any other source that makes you laugh. If you do laugh for any reason, judge yourself immediately and ask yourself if your laughter is justifiable. This should bring the laughing to an end quickly. If not, criticize how you laugh—is it too loud, too long, the wrong pitch or out of control?—so that you can lapse into an awkward silence.

How dangerous laughter can be for total unhappiness was amply demonstrated by Norman Cousins, author and the former editor of The Saturday Review. When he was diagnosed as having an incurable disease and was in great pain, Cousins decided to treat himself with laughter and rented funny movies such as Abbot and Costello and the Marx Brothers and laughed himself to health. (It is believed that laughter releases endorphins in the body which decrease pain.)

Just as laughter is contagious, so is seriousness. You can put a damper on any laughter with your seriousness. This will take some discipline because laughing feels good and exercises the entire body. One can laugh so hard one starts to cry. Can this possibly be good for you? Positively not!

Laughter is also thought to be a sign of being out of control or crazy. What will people think of you if you laugh too much? If you're not careful, laughter can sneak up on you when least expected and change your grimace to a grin. Always be on guard against it. Remember, you have the right to reject laughter. You don't have to go along with it. You can look at the person laughing and say, "What's so funny?" Laughter is usually irrational and illogical and sometimes both. Fight it off. It won't be easy. I am sure that with the help of this book, you can do it. If you don't laugh, then what? The next rule explains it. It's simple: complain a lot.

Exercises for Rule 19:

1. When was the last time you had a good deep belly laugh? Was it really necessary? Could you justify it on any rational basis?

2. If someone starts laughing around you, glare at him. If that won't stop him

immediately, leave the area. Laughing is infectious and there is no known antidote to it that really works in its presence.

3. Stay away from people who make you laugh. They are dangerous to your total unhappiness.

4. See if you can go through a day without laughing once. See if you can extend this to a week and then to a month.

5. See if you can reach a point where you can't remember the last time you had a good laugh.

Rule 20:
Complain as Much as Possible
wherever and whenever Possible

For total unhappiness there is nothing like complaining. It is the spice of unhappiness! No matter how well things may appear to be going in your life, you can always find something to complain about.

If you were nominated for a Nobel prize, you can still complain that this year's winners have not achieved that much, and you are not in good company. If you win an Academy Award, you can complain that it took so long for you to win it. You deserved it much earlier. If you win the lottery, you can complain about the taxes you'll have to pay on your winnings. When you get into Heaven, you can complain about the long line at the gate.

Complaining is a supreme way to stay unhappy. The more you gripe, the more you have to gripe about. You can always find someone to agree with you whole-heartedly no matter what you say, whether it be the sunny weather is bad for your skin, or your "ex" is a worthless person. Like laughter, complaining is contagious. You start complaining to someone and they will quickly join in, either complaining about what you are complaining about, or complaining about their own situation.

Another advantage of complaining over other roads to unhappiness is that it can be done anywhere. It requires no special equipment or company. You can start where you are. Since you're reading this book, complain about how stupid it is and why you even bothered with it in the first place. Certainly it costs too much. The author's style of writing is repetitious and pedantic. The exercises at the end of the Rules are ridiculous. Is the guy who wrote this book some kind of nut? And so on and so forth. There is no end to the possibilities of complaining.

Complaining can be quite subtle. One type of subtle complaint comes packaged in a sophisticated phrase called "constructive criticism." If someone asks for feedback, that's one thing, but when it is unsolicited, it is just faultfinding. Unsolicited "constructive criticism" is like "disparaging encouragement." You either build people up or tear them down. Complaining about how people do things is the way to tear them down. But before you complain about others, start with yourself. If you don't find anything wrong with your actions, you probably won't find anything wrong with others'. When reaching for profound unhappiness, a life without complaining would be unbearable.

Another subtle kind of complaining is called "objective reporting." However, it should really be called "enjoying the bad." Classic examples are news commentators who seem to get satisfaction out of reporting the bad news. Some of the real experts in this field are public radio newscasters. I love public radio newscasts and listen to them regularly, but it seems the news broadcasters take special delight in announcing that the unemployment rate went up by a whopping three-tenths of a percent. It could be argued that most news and newspaper stories are complaints about what is happening in the world. You never read in a newspaper that five-hundred planes landed safely at JFK airport and everyone had a boring trip. It doesn't sell papers. So draw your inspiration from these pundits and you'll never run out of things to complain about, no matter how trivial or insubstantial. Of course, you will have to decide what to complain about and that, in itself, leads to unhappiness. This is discussed in the next rule.

Exercise for Rule 20:

1. To master complaining, start right where you are. Suppose you are sitting in a chair reading this book. How does the chair feel? A little too soft? A little too hard? Is the chair a little lumpy? What is wrong with the chair? There must be something wrong with it. If it feels comfortable, look at the style of the chair. Is it too old-fashioned? Is it too modern? Is the style okay? What about the fabric? Is it too worn? Or too scratchy? What about the color? Is it a color you don't like? Is there another color you would prefer? Even if you like the color, how does it

not fit in with other things in the room? It doesn't match perfectly with all the other furniture in the room, does it? This is not a silent exercise. Complain loudly to whomever is in the room, "You know, Gladys, this chair is uncomfortable. I never have liked it since you bought it." If no one is in the room, phone someone and complain to them.

2. Complain about having to do all these exercises.

Rule 21:
Stay in a State of Indecision about as Much in Your Life as Possible

There is nothing so exhausting as being indecisive. Once a decision is made, no matter which way it is made, a tremendous amount of pressure is removed. Decision-making is stressful. Anyone who spends a day shopping can easily attest to having made innumerable decisions and considered various factors when choosing what to buy. Most people come home exhausted from shopping trips, although there is a small minority who seem to thrive on it. But for most of us, the act of deciding about which clothes or anything else to buy takes a heavy toll.

A marvelous way to maintain unhappiness is to be in a state of indecision as much as possible. So many factors must be weighed and so much information gathered before you can decide, you could make a mistake. If you do happen to decide about anything, "buyer's remorse" will bail you out.

As soon as the deal is consummated, the home buyer asks him/herself, "What have I done? My God, is this the house for me? In this neighborhood? Is it too small? Did I pay too much? How am I ever going to make the mortgage payments?" There is no end to the doubts and questions you can have about your decisions. Whatever you decided, you could have decided incorrectly. You are in a lose-lose situation. It is the perfect recipe for misery.

Remember the last time you bought something. It could be a big item such as a car or a more modest one such as a suit or dress. Carefully remember what happened within a few days of your purchase. The price dropped. Perhaps you bought a dress and two days later the same shop reduced it by 30 percent. If only you had waited a few more days. Those two words "if only" are magic for attaining total unhappiness. Remember that $800 answering machine you bought from a specialty electronics supplier thirty years ago? Well, if only you had waited thirty years, you could have bought one for $49 at any drugstore. If only you had sold your house when the market was at its height instead of waiting to sell in a sluggish market. If only you had bought your stock when it was low, instead of high. And if only you had not married Tom and waited until you met Dick or at least Harry. Always remember those two magic words: if only.

If it is your decision to purchase a new piece of equipment at work, bring it up at the next committee meeting. If no committee meeting is coming up, call a committee meeting. If you don't have a committee, it is never too late to form one. There is no mechanism quite as effective in postponing decisions as a committee. There everyone can bring up their concerns, and more information and research will be needed. Perhaps a subcommittee can be formed that will report back to the full committee. If you can get your decision firmly entrenched in the committee process, the decision has a good chance of being put off for years. In fact, social anthropologists theorize that the committee system led to the near extinction of Neanderthal man. The hunting committee couldn't make up their minds about where the woolly mammoth were. Neanderthal man was saved by a few renegades who refused to go to committee meetings and instead went hunting. And that's how we still have some Neanderthals with us today.

There is an even better way to stay totally unhappy. You probably didn't think it possible, but there is—and that is to know what you want to do and not do it. Procrastination is the subject of our next rule.

Exercise for Rule 21:

In your Personal Unhappiness Journal, make a list of all the things in your life you are presently in a state of indecision about. Next to each item, list what other factors must be considered before you decide. Picture the consequences in your life after each decision. What will happen to you if you buy Rice Krispies or Shredded Wheat? How will this affect you now, tonight, tomorrow morning at breakfast, five years from now? Evaluate each consequence carefully. No stone should be left unturned.

Rule 22:
Procrastinate

Before we go further, we must carefully distinguish between procrastination and indecision. Both keep you in murky waters, but procrastination adds an element of guilt which intensifies your uneasiness. When you are in a state of indecision, you feel that you do not have to act because you haven't come to a decision yet. You are still weighing the factors. If you decide, you then can regret your decision.

Procrastination is different from indecision because you know clearly what to do, but just don't do it. You are not indecisive about it. You want to clean up the garage to make it into a studio. It's clear that this is what you want to do. You just don't do it. You want to write the term paper that is due in two days. You don't write it. You want to get out of your relationship. It's not good and hasn't been good for years. You don't get out. You want to start exercising because you are out of shape, but you don't. You know that you haven't had your teeth checked or cleaned by a dentist in two years and you should go, but you don't. In these cases you know what you want to do. You are not suffering from indecision. You gain despondency by the guilt you create by not doing what you want to do. Of course, the longer you procrastinate, the more guilty you become. If anyone challenges your procrastination, brag about it. Don't decrease your total unhappiness by forgiving yourself for your procrastination or indecision. This is the next rule.

Exercise for Rule 22:

Mull over all the things you have been procrastinating about. Do not make a list of them. You can make a list later.

Rule 23:
Forgive No One in Your Life for Anything They Did or Did Not Do to You. The Most Important Person You Should Not Forgive is Yourself

It is always best to keep your wounds open and bleeding. Forgiveness is a salve that helps stop the bleeding and heal the wound. For total unhappiness, you want none of that. All the things your parents did to you should not be forgotten or forgiven. Neither should the things your children did to you. As Clarence Darrow aptly remarked, "The first half of our lives is ruined by our parents and the second half by our children." Why should we forgive any of them for all the wrongs they did to us?

I would not suggest for a moment that you take the cynical view of Oscar Wilde who suggested, "Always forgive your enemies—nothing annoys them so much." Not forgiving your "ex" for all the wrongs he or she did to you keeps bitterness in your soul that is absolutely exquisite. This applies equally to all people and events that have wronged you. But the one person who is essential that you not forgive is yourself. Not forgiving others is mere child's play compared to not forgiving yourself. By not forgiving yourself about your life, your unhappiness is carried right up front where you and everyone else can clearly see it.

Self-criticism is essential to achieve unhappiness. You are your own worst enemy. No one is as good a critic of you as yourself. You've had a whole life to practice. Never give it up! Don't let yourself get away with anything! If you can't make a decision, beat yourself up about it. If you are a procrastinator, never forgive that fact. If your schedule is too busy with little rhythm in your daily and weekly activities, be critical of it.

Show no compassion for yourself. Compassion for yourself is the most powerful healer and an enemy of becoming and staying brutally unhappy. Lack of forgiveness towards yourself and others creates permanent hostility that pollutes the environment. Everyone will sense it. It cannot be hidden. As the saying goes, "All people make us happy, some when they come and some when they go." By never forgiving yourself and others, you will make others happy when you leave. Chronically angry people have this wonderful facility. You will also know you are on the right path when people avoid you altogether. It is time to go from general to specific rules in order to create total unhappiness. The next rule deals with diet.

Exercises for Rule 23:

1. In your Personal Unhappiness Journal, list all of the things your parents, spouse, ex-spouse, children, relatives, friends, acquaintances, business associates and God did to you or failed to do for you. Do not forgive them.

2. Remember your mistakes and sundry faux pas. Take time to go over each and every one. Savor the regret you feel as you wish you had done this or decide you should have done that. Obsess about your unhappy life because of what you have or have not done.

3. Contemplate the terrible hand you were dealt and how little you have to be grateful for.

Rule 24:
Eat a High Fat Diet.
Let Things Eat You

Fat has been implicated as one of the leading causes of heart disease, cancer, adult-onset diabetes, and many other diseases. The fact that one of three Americans gets cancer should not surprise anyone when they consider Americans eat a diet in which 36 percent of the calories consumed come from fat.

For total unhappiness, it is hard to beat cancer with its radiation and chemotherapy treatments, loss of hair, nausea, endless tests and decisions about treatment. However, heart disease also leads to severe unhappiness. You can have triple bypass surgery at a cost of over $40,000. If you continue on the high fat diet after the operation, there is a very good chance that your arteries will again clog up and you can again be unhappy. You will be concerned each time your heart takes a beat if it's going to take another, and about whether the intense pain will return.

You will, of course, need to be exceptionally patient eating a high fat diet, as it takes years before diseases take hold. It is amazing that we stay well as long as we do before getting these illnesses. The body is an incredible machine. But in the long run, a high fat diet brings you excess weight, chronic illness and unhappiness.

In the short run, it's not so much what you eat, but what eats you. If you are continually under stress, or are worrying incessantly about what's happening or not happening in your life, you can eat the best food and still become ill in a short time. When you are constantly angry, sad or depressed, you do not properly digest your food. Therefore, in the short run, try to keep your level of stress as high as possible. You should always discuss your problems while eating. This way you're sure to have indigestion and discomfort following the meal.

Another thing you can do is to eat huge quantities at each meal, especially of meat.

Since meat takes hours to digest, eating it in large quantities increases the possibility of getting indigestion, heartburn and other discomforts. There have been many people who, after colossally high fat meals, had indigestion so severe they thought they were having a heart attack and went to the hospital. A few days and several thousand dollars later, the conclusion was reached that it was not a heart attack but a stomachache. Remember, when you eat huge amounts of food at any meal, you might have to wait a few minutes for the pain to set in.

Here are some other pointers about unhappiness and eating. Whenever possible, try eating standing up. Recall that "time is money," and you lack time. If you must sit down to eat, the least you can do is eat while driving, because then you're not just wasting your time eating, you're going somewhere. This is becoming the new trend. I am sure that future social anthropologists will be able to analyze our diet by closely examining the fibers of our cars' upholstery and floor mats. I know they could do that in my car. I understand that the various holders for cups and trays in cars has now become a big selling point. It is only a matter of time before the glove compartment is replaced by a mini-microwave oven—so we can warm up our old hamburgers as we drive.

If you're going to sit down at a table to eat, the least you can do is eat as fast as possible and chew as little as possible. You have important things to say and better things to do than to chew your food. Thank God your mother isn't around to remind you to chew! If you're lucky enough, you can join the 4,000 Americans who achieve total unhappiness instantly each year by dying of "food inhalation." They choke to death trying to swallow a large piece of food, usually a piece of meat.

A great adjunct to a high fat diet, or eating huge meals, or worrying and being angry so you can't digest your food, is to avoid exercise. This will be discussed next.

Exercises for Rule 24:

1. To increase the stress in your life, try arguing at the dinner table. If you live alone, open up your bills. At breakfast, try balancing your checkbook. Pay your bills while eating lunch.

2. Never leave a meal until you feel totally stuffed. Who knows when you will eat again? Nothing is certain in this world.

Rule 25:
Exercise as Little as Possible, and If You Decide to Exercise, Pick Something that You Distinctly Don't Like Doing

I t is imperative that you do as little exercise as possible throughout your life, especially as you get older. A lack of exercise is even more important for complete unhappiness than eating high fat food. Together, however, they can't be beat. Exercise gets your blood circulating; this brings the nutrients and oxygen to all parts of your body. In sustained exercise, your body also releases certain chemicals, called endorphins, which make you feel good. If you're feeling depressed and you take a half-hour walk, you will feel better.

For uncompromising distress, naturally you want to remain exactly where you are, miserable. Although it has been conclusively proven that the effects of aging can be positively altered by any person devoting just a couple hours a week to exercise, you are quite aware that exercise is dangerous to your health. When you see these crazy people jogging up and down asphalt streets, you wonder if the American Medical Association brought this craze into being to increase their business. In fact, the whole field of sports medicine has grown up, not from treating super athletes like Joe Montana, but from treating the average Joe who is continually injuring his knees, ankles, or shins running on asphalt. Moreover, the entire physical therapy profession has blossomed from this craze. Why take a chance and hurt yourself when you can just sit around and watch TV?

If you don't do any exercise, you will never know how out of shape you are because you never put your body to the test. Why walk a block if you can drive your car? That's what cars are for, right? Why climb a flight of stairs when you can take an elevator? That's what elevators are there for. What you will learn is that the less exercise you do, the less you will be able to do.

It is never too late to stop all exercise. Once you stop doing any exercise and putting your bones and muscle to any test, they become weaker. One day, someone whose only exercise for the last decade has been jumping to conclusions, will break their hip bone and then fall down. Most people think that the person falls down and then breaks their bone, due to the impact of the fall. Sure, this happens, but it also happens that hips break first because they are extremely fragile, due to osteoporosis.

Osteoporosis is an epidemic among older American women. One of the main causes is that the bones have not been put under stress. Simple exercise such as vigorous walking puts your bones under stress. For misery in the later years, the less you exercise when young, the greater the chance you will have to develop osteoporosis and other crippling diseases when you get older.

You become less flexible as you get older, so you will have to be more careful when exercising at all. This is especially important when you start to feel minor aches and pains. When any minor aches or pains start, stop your exercise program! Don't do anything on any day you feel less than perfect. You will find that you exercise less and less and soon stop altogether. Be sure to ignore what an eighty-year-old golfer told my friend one day during a golf game. He said, "If I did not go out to play golf every time I had an ache or pain, I would not have played any golf for the last thirty years."

If you are younger and considering starting an exercise program, I have one suggestion that you can incorporate into any exercise program and still achieve total unhappiness. That is to select an activity and a setting that you do not like. If you're a person who likes the outdoors and quiet, join an indoor health club where they play loud rock music all day. Additionally, start a weight training program. You'll find that despite getting help setting up a program from a physical fitness counselor, you'll race through the routine without taking enough time between sets because you really don't like the place and want to get it over with. Before long you will injure yourself and discontinue going altogether. I know. I did it twice. Picking something you don't like and doing it because it's "good" for you is a wonderful way to perpetuate your unhappiness.

With regard to time, remember Ben Franklin's dictum that "time is money." Can you afford the time to exercise? Of course not. Ignore the Chinese saying that those who won't make time for exercise will have to make time for illness. Select a form of exercise that you won't do because it's expensive and takes too much time— perhaps skydiving. Remember, for total unhappiness on your busy schedule, you may think you'd like to do some exercise, but you just don't have the time.

Another excellent way to achieve lasting melancholy is to believe you have to be good at what you do rather than just have fun doing it. Dancing is a wonderful example of this. There is probably no better exercise and fun than dancing. It can be any type of dancing from rock and roll to square dancing to swing to African. To become a good dancer takes practice. Do not even attempt to dance because you're not good enough and you don't have the confidence to try it. Absolutely shun the idea that practice or taking a dance class will increase your confidence. This is important in many areas of your life, but especially about fun things like dancing. If there's anything you don't need for total unhappiness, it's an evening out dancing.

One last point: any exercise requires an act of will. When you feel the urge, recall the words of Robert M. Hutchins, former president of the University of Chicago, "Whenever I get the urge to exercise, I lay down until the feeling passes." (Hutchins eliminated football at the University in 1939.) If the feeling still doesn't go away, call a friend and discuss the dangers of exercise and all the people you know who have injured themselves exercising. As you grow older, any ache or pain in your body is a definite signal to cut out all exercise. I am happy to report for total unhappiness only eight percent of Americans exercise enough to have any impact on their own aging process. Since most exercise occurs in an outdoor setting, this brings up the dangers of being outside, at all. This is discussed in the next rule.

Exercises for Rule 25:

1. Whenever you contemplate undertaking exercise, refer back to the Rule on Procrastination.

2. Buy a exercise/health magazine. Take notice of the bodies of the men and women in the photographs. Are these the bodies of real people? Not on your life. These are the bodies of people who have had plastic surgery or take steroids.

This is not for you. Picture how silly you would look in an exercise outfit or working out in a gym next to one of these guys or gals.

3. If you're not presently in an exercise program, great! You do not have to do any more exercises.

4. If you feel you should do some exercise, make a list of five types of exercise you distinctly dislike. Rank them from one to five, five being the one you like least and one being the most tolerable. Start doing No. 5 on a regular basis.

5. If older, and older in this case means you're older if you know anyone who is younger, stop any exercise whenever you feel any ache or pain. I am not referring to sharp intense pains which are an indication to stop an activity—pains that many runners have learned to ignore and have subsequently done serious injury to themselves. These runners, however, have achieved total unhappiness as they could

no longer continue their running activities afterwards.

6. Avoid all kinds of exercise in everyday life. Plan your day so you can drive instead of walk. Park as close as you can to where you are going. It is best to circle the block several times looking for the closest parking spot.

7. Avoid climbing stairs whenever possible—including curbs.

8. Whenever you think of taking a walk or walking anywhere, sit down, or better yet, lay down and ask yourself if this walk is really necessary. You will usually find that it isn't.

Rule 26:
Stay as Far Away from Nature as You Can

Whenever possible you should stay indoors. Keep your shades drawn and especially try to avoid letting morning sun enter your home. It tends to lift your spirits. Keep your windows shut. Make sure all the pollutants in your home are not disturbed by any breezes.

When you leave your home or work place, go directly to your car and don't roll down your window. Do not take any sort of excursions into nature. Be especially careful to avoid the ocean or any large body of water. The ocean gives off negative ions which uplift your spirits. For similar reasons, stay away from the mountains. The air in mountains also gives off negative ions and could inspire you. It is best not to take any trips to forests. As President Reagan so adroitly put it, "If you've seen one redwood tree, you've seen them all." All these natural places are dangerous to your downcast feelings. Being in nature, breathing in the fresh air and being in these pristine environments, all tend to dispel distress. Therefore, avoid them. Once you start taking excursions into nature, they can become habit forming. A habit like being in nature can wreak havoc to your misery.

If you somehow do get stuck in nature, whatever else you do, do not take off your shoes and socks. It just feels too good. Remember, walking barefoot on the ocean's edge exposes your feet to all sorts of dangers such as sand crabs and broken shells. Besides the danger, it is too cold in a northern climate or too hot in a southern one. Needless to say, never immerse your whole body in water. That is something just for kids. If you're barefoot in a grassy area, remember there might be all sorts of insects in the grass. Moreover, your feet could get wet, and you might get a fungal infection. Bear in mind, if God wanted you to go barefoot why did S/He give you shoes?

Staying inside also has the advantage of keeping you in contact with positive ions, the ions that make you feel bad. But remember they are positive. So by staying continually indoors you have something positive in your life on a continuous basis. Never open your windows. Stuffy air is great for keeping all these positive ions in, as well as for maintaining your forlorn state. Try to do as much as possible indoors and as little as possible out-of-doors. If you must have some outdoors, watch it on television.

Some people make a point of being in nature for a part of each day, even if it is a short morning walk or eating lunch in a park. Often, city parks are located near places of work in most cities. Even a small dose of nature like this should be avoided. You must conquer, use, and exploit nature, not appreciate it. If you can't do this, the least you can do is ignore it.

Walking should be avoided at all costs. Do not let anyone lead you to believe that taking a walk in your neighborhood park is worth the bother. You should only consider taking an expensive safari into nature. When you return, it leaves you with the feeling that you need another vacation. Small experiences such as a half-hour walk in your nearby park aren't worthwhile. It's either all or nothing. Since you can't do it "right," why bother? This attitude is wonderful for creating and maintaining total unhappiness. Another thing to remember is that anytime you go outside, there is a chance of injury and the pain that goes with it. This is discussed in the next rule.

Exercises for Rule 26:

1. Survey your home. Remove any house plants or fresh flowers. Think of your allergies.

2. Take notice of all the crime that has occurred outside of your home in the last month. If you don't know of any, check with your neighbors. If they don't know of any, keep checking with others until you find someone who can tell you of crime in your neighborhood. It just isn't safe to go outside of your home, even during the daytime. Stay inside and be safe.

3. In your Personal Unhappiness Journal, list all of the local parks near your home and work. Include your backyard. Avoid going to any of them. What could be more boring than going to a nearby park or your own backyard?

Rule 27:
Believe Absolutely that There Should Be No Pain or Suffering of Any Kind in Your Life

This is a tricky rule, but I feel sure you can handle it. There is usually pain and suffering in all of our lives; it just takes different forms. For some of us, it is our own physical pain. For some, it is the physical pain of someone close to them. And for some, there are all sorts of social pains. It is hard to avoid it.

The key to your unhappiness is not whether pain exists in one form or another, but how you handle it. If you say "yes" to your universe, it enables you to accept what life has given you. Although you might not like some of its aspects, you can still be happy. Obviously for total unhappiness, you must not accept any pain in your life. You must say "no" to the universe and continually fight against what life has given you. People who say "yes" to their universe might also be trying to change things, but their attitude will be different. By saying "no" to your universe, you become bitter, create suffering, and feel you are a victim of circumstance; life just isn't fair. "Why me!" Feeling like a victim is wonderful for creating inconsolable misery.

Demand that there be no pain in your life—but always look for it. If your body or your social relations are pain-free at the moment, look around the world and find pain somewhere else. For example, you can demand that all Catholics and Protestants in Northern Ireland love each other before you can be happy. If, by some miracle, that happened, your happiness could depend on every Hindu and Moslem loving each other. And if that also happened, you could demand that every Jew come to love every Arab and vice versa in the Middle East. It never ends. This is perfect for unhappiness because pain and suffering are always present somewhere.

Gurjieff, the 20th century Russian philosopher and mystic, claimed the last thing people are willing to give up is their suffering, despite all their protests to the contrary. Milton Berle, himself Jewish, once observed that the reason Jews don't drink much alcohol is that drinking interferes with their suffering.

It is through their suffering that most people maintain their identities. Without their suffering, people would not know who they were. Who would you be? It's entirely logical, only a fool would be happy in this world.

Exercises for Rule 27:

1. Feel all your bodily aches and pains. Determine that you cannot be happy until all these have been completely eliminated. Reposition yourself so you can feel more uncomfortable. Try to maintain this uncomfortable position for as long as possible. Suffer. Suffer. Suffer.

2. Make a list of all local, state, national and international problems. If you can't think of any problem areas, read a newspaper. Determine that you cannot be happy until all of these problems have been eliminated.

Rule 28:
Believe the World You See is the Only World There is.
Logic is Always the Answer.

Reality is simple. It is everything you see in front of you. It is everything you read in your local newspaper. There are no other levels of reality other than what you can see with your own eyes, read in the newspaper or see on TV. Everything else is pure poppycock or the fuzzy wuzzy stuff of these New Age space cadets and religious fanatics. If you can't see God, there is no God. What could be more obvious than that? You don't have to be an Albert Einstein to figure that out. You're not stupid, right? You're not going to be taken in by naive spiritual concepts about God and higher powers. Not if you want to be unhappy. Isn't religion the opiate of the people? If you believe only what you can see and read in the newspaper, then you can stay miserable.

Deny your intuition. Never listen to the inner voice that guides you without rational justification. Instead make lists of the reasons to take or not take action. If the list is overwhelming in one direction and you do not feel right about it, that doubt is your intuition. That intuition comes from your heart and the right side of your brain.

The heart has reasons only the heart knows. The right side of your brain is not logical, unlike the left side where all the logical deductions come from. For perfect unhappiness, it is essential to deny your intuition and rely constantly on your rational mind.

Say you go to look at an apartment. Your rational mind wants to rent it, but your intuition doesn't feel right about it. That night you don't sleep well. Something is bothering you, but you just can't pinpoint what's wrong with the apartment. You can't defend your position on a rational basis, so why try? Always be logical. Logic is what you can list on a sheet of paper, what you can see with your eyes. Your intuition just knows. For unhappiness, don't believe those who say logic is good for the mind but not for the guts.

Women seem to be more in touch with their intuition. Most men are rational. Anyone's intuition can develop if they trust it. If you want unhappiness, don't trust anything you can't see or explain on a rational basis.

We are nearing the 21st century. You do not have time for superstitious things that we cannot see, whether it be a higher power or your own intuition. Intuition is for fools. Naturally, the same thing applies, even more so, to any belief in a higher power. You must realize that, in truth, you are alone. This is discussed in the next rule.

Exercises for Rule 28:

1. In your Personal Unhappiness Journal, list all of the times you followed your heart rather than your head. What was wrong about these decisions?

2. Make a list of all the times you followed your head and not your heart. What was right about these decisions?

3. When any new decision comes up in your life, always follow your head, not your heart. Do this regardless of how the answers to the above two questions turned out. Never trust your feelings!

Rule 29:
Always Remember How Lonely You Are. Feel How Separate You Are from Others

It does not matter whether you are living alone or with others. You should always feel that you are lonely and separate. To be really miserable, you should feel that the company of others intensifies your loneliness. Know that there is no one to turn to with your problems. Acknowledge that people aren't interested in listening to you and your problems because you're not interested in listening to their problems.

This feeling of loneliness can be expanded to all sorts of situations. If you are at a social gathering, do not try to start a conversation with anyone you do not already know. No one really wants to talk with you anyway, and you have nothing to say. The less you try to make contact with others, the more alone you feel and the more miserable you become. Besides, making contact with others involves some risk, and risk means leaving your normal "unhappiness comfort zone" and experiencing some unusual uneasiness. You don't need this type of uneasiness when you can be unhappy without any contact with anyone. After some practice you will feel lonely and separate whether by yourself or surrounded by people. This brings up the last rule which is that you have no control over how you feel.

Exercises for Rule 29:

1. Make a list of the times within the last week you said something to someone who you didn't already know. (Even a comment to a checkout clerk at your grocery store counts.) If your answer is more than one time, see if you can decrease that number by half in the next week. If your answer was none, keep it up.

2. Make a list of the times within the last month you said something to someone you didn't already know. Follow the instructions as with No. 1.

3. When you last felt lonely, did you make any effort to contact anyone? If the answer is "yes," try avoiding that the next time you feel lonely. If the answer was "no," keep it up. It's just a matter of practice to always feel you are alone. The more lonely you feel, the more unhappy you will become.

Rule 30:
Acknowledge that You Have No Choice Whether to Be Happy or Unhappy. It All Depends on the Circumstances in Your Life and is Completely Outside of Your Control

It is critical to always keep in mind that you have no choice. Given your circumstances, anyone else in your shoes would be unhappy, too. If anyone else had your illnesses and what you have to go through in your hard life, you can bet that they would be miserable, too. If anyone else had the job you have and all you have to put up with including your hard-driving boss, uncooperative fellow workers, long hours, and insecurity of even holding the job, they would be crestfallen, too. What other choice would they have?

If someone had to have neighbors such as yours—inconsiderate and abusing your space with loud music; always blocking your driveway; refusing to mow their lawn; cluttering their yard, which detracts from the appearance of your home and lowers real estate values—he or she would be inconsolable, too. What other choice would he or she have? Anyone who had your parents would be unhappy. Wow, how could he or she be anything but unhappy?

With your father and your mother, no way!

Abe Lincoln's comment, "Most folks are about as happy as they make up their minds to be," is just a load of hogwash. It was easy for Lincoln to say that. He was born in a log cabin; his mother died when he was nine years old. His father didn't believe in "book" learning and Lincoln went to school scarcely a year. As an adult, he entered the grocery business which failed, leaving him a large debt. The first woman he courted died, the second promptly rejected his marriage proposal, the third whom he married bore him four sons. The second-born died one month before his fourth birthday. While Lincoln was President, the two youngest contracted typhoid fever, and his third-born son died of it at age eleven.

Lincoln lost his first bid for a seat in the Illinois State Legislature. He was unsuccessful in his first two attempts to obtain his party's nomination to run for the House of Representatives. He lost the election for a U.S. Senate seat.

As President, the generals under his command refused to engage the Confederacy and follow Lincoln's orders. Lincoln became so frustrated with General McClellan's inaction that he observed "that if General McClellan did not want to use the army, he would like to borrow it." (When Lincoln finally found a general who was willing to fight, Ulysses S. Grant, he was informed that Grant drank and was advised to remove him. "Do you know what brand of whiskey?" Lincoln asked. "I'd like to send a barrel to each of my other generals.")

Lincoln had no friends in the White House, suffered from ill health (his hands and feet were always cold), he had bad corns on his feet, and while President he was stricken with variola, a mild form of smallpox. He hardly ate, slept poorly, and had ominous dreams. He was harshly criticized by the press and his looks and physical demeanor were ridiculed in cartoons. Members of his own cabinet showed disrespect toward him. Therefore, it is easy to see how Lincoln could say, "Man is about as happy as he makes up his mind to be."

If Lincoln had your background, your education, your hardships, your disabilities, your job, your kids and especially your parents, you can bet "your bottom dollar" (if you haven't already lost it) he would be singing another tune. Let no one persuade you otherwise that you have any choice in how you feel about your life. The simple truth is that you are totally unhappy through no fault of your own. It is completely out of your control. You were doomed at birth. Your unhappiness is irreversible. It is your fate. If you remember this and always keep it in the forefront of your mind, you too can become and stay forever Totally Unhappy in a Peaceful World.

Exercises for Rule 30:

1. In your Personal Unhappiness Journal, list all of the factors that are outside of your control regarding the present situation in your life, including, but not limited to:
   a. Your family
   b. Your job
   c. Your home
   d. Your finances
   e. Your future
   f. The World

2. Do the mirror exercise. (We started Rule No. 1 with a mirror exercise, and it is only "fitting and proper" that the last exercise be a mirror one, too.) Look into a mirror, preferably one that has a big crack running through it. If you're stuck with a crackless mirror, take a hammer and crack it. Keep looking in the mirror until you feel totally unhappy. After reading this book, it probably won't take that much time. Say out loud:

"I am totally unhappy, and I plan to stay that way the rest of my life. This is no fault of mine, and it is completely out of my control."

Say this again and again until you believe it. Check the mirror and make sure there is a big frown on your face. Do not leave home until this is firmly entrenched in your mind and a big frown covers your face.

Final Examination

To see if you have mastered the principles, test yourself with the final exam. Ultimately, your feelings of being permanently unhappy will replace any exam, but until you have that feeling, this exam will help you on the way.

1. The reason you should never forgive your parents for anything they did or did not do to you is:
    a. They did it intentionally to louse up your life.
    b. They never really loved you.
    c. They never had your best interests at stake.
    d. All of the above.

2. The reason never to do any exercise is:
    a. It often leads to injuries.
    b. You're too busy.
    c. Exercise is boring.
    d. All of the above.

3. The reason to stay inside as much as possible is:
   a. There are too many undesirables outside, such as your neighbors.
   b. There is too much crime.
   c. The sun is just too bright or the sky is just too gray.
   d. All of the above.

4. The best reason for staying in a state of indecision is:
   a. You don't have to take any action.
   b. There is always more information that you can gather.
   c. You could make a mistake.
   d. All of the above.

5. The reason to complain whenever possible is:
   a. It gives you something to say.
   b. It helps you focus on what is wrong.
   c. It makes conversation flow more easily.
   d. All of the above.

6. The reason everything is to be taken so seriously is:
   a. Everything is serious.
   b. You read your daily newspaper.
   c. You are a realist.
   d. All of the above.

7. The reason you are totally unhappy is because of:
   a. The circumstances in your life.
   b. The parents you have.
   c. The children you have or don't have.
   d. All of the above.

8. The reason to stay as far away from nature as possible is:
   a. The outdoors is a place in which you can get injured.
   b. All the "negative" ions.
   c. It is bad for your allergies.
   d. All of the above.

9. The reason your children, if you have any, act the way they do is:
   a. They know it will upset you.
   b. They know it will upset you.

c. They know it will upset you.

d. All of the above.

Since all the above answers to the final exam are correct, you have achieved a 100% score, no matter which alternatives you selected. You are well on your way to total unhappiness. Keep it up.

The Final Summary

Part of your problem is that you may have thought being happy was your goal. In fact, quite to the contrary, your goal in life is the opposite, to be unhappy. This was the main problem that I had to overcome. It took me years to realize and many repeated lessons to learn that what I really wanted in life was to be totally unhappy. Once I understood this, my whole attitude changed. I learned to be an expert at being unhappy. Subsequently, I started to see the underlying principles, and it has been the purpose of this book to share these principles with you. I hope I have succeeded.

The Joys of Unhappiness

Congratulations. You read a part or the whole of this book. (Or perhaps you immediately turned to this page.) For your efforts, you are entitled to know the joys of unhappiness. It is said that in every strength exists a weakness, and in every weakness exists a strength. The strength in unhappiness is that you will live your life in the same atmosphere with most everyone else you know. You will have a limitless camaraderie with almost everyone in your life and almost everyone you meet. Although each person may be unhappy for a different reason, you will be able to share your unhappiness with each other and have much to commiserate, whether it be lousy relationships, terrible financial situations or medical woes.

Happy people can be very irritating. After saying "This is a beautiful day," whether it is or not, what can happy people really talk about? If they find out you are deep in debt and considering bank-ruptcy, the happy person says to you, "That will be an interesting challenge." Do you want to hear this? If you develop a disease and don't think you have much time left, do you want to hear from a happy person that "Now you can appreciate each day you have left to the fullest." What has been pointed out about saints also applies to happy people: they are very hard to have around. The only disadvantage of being unhappy is that you don't feel good and think you'd like to feel better. If you can get over this slight drawback, a full life of total unhappiness can really open up for you.

The weakness in being happy is that happy people have a lot of trouble finding people who are also happy. One recent study found that only two percent of our population wakes up happy each day. Luckily, a happy person who is around an unhappy person long enough will eventu-ally shed their happiness and become unhappy. It is much easier for an unhappy person to bring a happy person down than for a happy person to bring an unhappy person up. Unhappiness just has a much greater heaviness, and like gravity, tends to bring everything around it down. Once the happy person starts to feel unhappy, he or she will have much more to talk about with other people than ever before. The true joy of unhappiness can also be theirs.

The only advantage that happy people have is that they feel good. Feeling good about themselves makes them feel good about others and the world around them. Thankfully, there are very few happy people left in the world. It has been suggested that happy people be placed on the endangered species list. It may be that happy people are now totally extinct, at least in America. We unhappy people cannot say we are sorry to see them go.

A Peaceful World

As to the question of whether or not it is a peaceful world, if you have followed all the previous rules and become a totally unhappy person, then the question is academic, isn't it? If you're totally unhappy, what difference does it make what the world outside you is like? You will take your unhappiness wherever you go. It doesn't matter if you are in the Garden of Eden, you will still feel unhappy. As Samuel Hoffenstein, author of the long-forgotten *Poems in Praise of Practically Nothing* and a true connoisseur of unhappiness observed, "Wherever I go, I go too, and spoil everything." Therefore, it is how you think and feel that determines what you perceive. It is not the other way around, as most people think. The reality of your life is an internal phenomenon that is projected onto the outside. This has been said many times by innumerable philosophers.

The outer world of circumstances shapes itself to the inner world of thought. . . . Circumstances does not make the man; it reveals him to himself. . . . Man, as the lord and master of thought, is the maker of himself, and the author of his environment.
—James Allen

There is no reality except the one within us. That is why so many people live such an unreal life. They take the images outside of them for reality and never allow the world within to assert itself.
—Herman Hesse

The fountain of content must spring up in the mind, and he who has so little knowledge of human nature as to seek happiness by changing anything but his own disposition will waste his life in fruitless efforts and multiply the grief he proposes to remove.
—Samuel Johnson

Even if you disagree with these maxims and think the world is not a peaceful one, you still must admit that even if it were totally peaceful, it would not make any difference to you if you are unhappy. If you are unhappy and take a vacation to a supposedly "happy" place, this trip won't make you happy. The problem is always, as Hoffenstein points out, that you took yourself along and "spoiled everything." The world will always be a reflection of the way you think. If you are totally unhappy, then the world will be a totally unhappy place. Since I started this book quoting Milton, it is appropriate that I conclude it with him. Milton said, in Paradise Lost:

> The mind is its own place, and in itself
> Can make a Heav'n of Hell, or a Hell of Heav'n.

The Unhappy Newsletter

Even after reading this entire book and studiously carrying out the exercises, you may still backslide occasionally into happiness. It could happen unexpectedly, when for example, something that you expected would be disastrous turned out to be quite nice, and all your worrying was for nothing. Or perhaps you overcame a difficulty in your life, rather than avoiding it. When these unexpected moments of happiness come into your life, you can be thrown off your unhappiness path unless you make preparations and have regular reminders to keep you on track.

There can be no better reminder to stay on your path to total unhappiness than to receive "The Unhappy Newsletter." It contains all sorts of information that insures total unhappiness. There are hot tips on how to lose your money through investments; a column entitled "The Disease of the Month and How to Get It," which is a great source for worrying about illness in your-self, your loved ones, or at least someone you know; a "Dear Gil" column where I'll answer your questions and guide you towards total unhappiness; and finally, more rules, exercises, tests and affirmations to keep you in shape for profound and deep melancholy.

"The Unhappy Newsletter" is a must to stay on the path. There are four issues a year, coming out at irregular times. The irregularity will help keep you on your unhappy toes because you will never know when "The Unhappy Newsletter" will cross your mail box. It will come in a brown paper wrapper so no one can know your true path or understand why you act as you do.

Become a charter subscriber of "The Unhappy Newsletter" for $99.95 a year. Priced to promote your unhappiness—unhappiness doesn't come cheap. After receiving the Newsletter and finding you are not happy with it, well that's just more grist for the mill on your path to total unhappiness. There are no full or even partial refunds. A totally unhappy readership is my goal.

As an extra bonus for becoming a charter subscriber of "The Unhappy Newsletter," you can buy for a mere $4.95 "The Unhappy Can Opener." This can opener looks like a simple manual can opener except that it doesn't work. In fact, it is guaranteed not to work. Now, if there is anything that can bring about instant unhappiness quicker than starting to open a can with a can opener that won't work, let me know. Perhaps I'll use your suggestion in a future issue. So check the box below to get your "Unhappy Can Opener." This unhappy can opener offer is open only to the first million unhappy people who order, so act today.

As to payment for the charter subscription to "The Unhappy Newsletter," as all totally unhappy people do, I sometimes trust in God, but all others pay cash. Your payment must be made in either U.S. Postal Service money orders or cash through Western Union. You will receive no acknowledgment of your receipt. Eventually you will wonder about mail fraud and start inquiring with the Post Office and experience the unhappiness of dealing with a federal bureaucracy and a bureaucrat who has helped many people along the way on the path to total unhappiness. After all this has happened, "The Unhappy Newsletter" will appear suddenly in your mail box. Oh, unhappy days! Don't delay. You are a guaranteed loser. All you have to do is subscribe to "The Unhappy Newsletter." You have nothing to gain and everything to lose, at least $99.95 and more if you want "The Unhappy Can Opener." Act now. Your misery depends on it.

For a one year subscription (four issues), mail your U.S. Postal Money Order or cash through Western Union to: (Personal checks not accepted)

The Unhappy Newsletter
Timbuktu

Check if you want "The Unhappy Can Opener" and enclose an additional $4.95, plus $9.95 for shipping and handling, making a total of $14.90 for the can opener (small print always leads to unhappiness). Expect delivery in 2 to 5 years. Unhappiness guaranteed!

Please print

Name:_____

Street:_____

City: _____ State: ____

Zip: _____

Daytime phone: _____

Evening Phone: _____

Age: ___ Sex: _____ Height: _____

Weight: _____ Hair color: _____

Father's favorite sport:_____

Mother's favorite ice cream flavor: _____

Father's favorite ice cream: _____

Mother's favorite sport: _____

Your favorite position in sex:

a. Above _____   b. Below _____

c. Sideways _____

d. It's been so long, I don't remember _____

e. All of the above _____

f. None of the above _____

Nickname you were called as a child that you despise and wish never to be called again: _____
Your favorite way to make yourself totally unhappy: _____

_____

_____

_____

_____

_____

_____

_____

_____

_____

_____

_____

_____

_____

Please use as many additional pages as you need to complete this question. (Your answer to this question might appear in "The Unhappy Newsletter." Legal names will be omitted. If I use your "favorite way," I shall identify you by your nickname only.)

Note: Any subscription form not completely filled in will be returned.

Books by Gil Friedman (who else?)

How to be Totally Unhappy in a Peaceful World @ $11.95

A Dictionary of Love @ $11.95.

"...a terrific book. Over 600 quotes from more than 300 people cover just about every perspective on love, and through them all the voice of experience is clearly heard. Funny, rueful, practical, wise and compassionate, this collection is a recommended gift to anyone who might be in a love relationship.... In other words a lot of people would enjoy and benefit from this book. One charming feature is the great range of attitudes displayed. One can disagree totally with one, and on the same page find one that rings true and provides an insight. Lots of fun, and more educational than many a tome."

—New Age Retailer

"There is either a good laugh or a real thought-provoker (or even both) on each page."

—New England Bride

The above are excepts from two of over fifteen favorable reviews. False modesty prevents me from quoting them all.

Library Motel @ $25.00.
A novel concerning relationships and marijuana. A spiral-bound 8-1/2" by 11" paperback. A limited edition. Don't miss it!

How to Buy and Sell a Used Car in Europe @ $5.95.
This is a 24-page booklet originally published in 1971 with 1977, 1985 and 1990 addenda. It deals primarily with buying used cars in Germany, but contains useful information about buying used cars in other countries of western Europe. Recommended in Harvard Student Agency books, "Let's Go Europe," "Let's Go France," "Let's Go Switzerland & Austria." Just what your grandmother needs!

How to Order

Send orders to:
Gil Friedman
PO Box 1063
Arcata, CA 95518-1063
(707) 822-5001

Name _____

Address _____

City _____ **State** _____ **Zip** _____

Please send me the following books. Unlike "The Unhappy Newsletter," I understand that I may return any books for a full refund, no questions asked.

Quantity	Book	Total

Total of above books: $____

$2.00 first item; $.50 each additional.
Canada add $2.00 per order;
Foreign orders add $3.00   **Shipping**: $____

California addresses add 7.25% **Sales Tax**: $____

Send Check/Money Order   **Grand Total**: $____